THE CLASSIC
Rolls-Royce

THE CLASSIC
Rolls-Royce

G. N. GEORGANO

Distributed by
Frederick Fell Publishers, Inc.
386 Park Avenue South
New York, N.Y. 10016

First Published in 1983 by
Bison Books Corp.
17 Sherwood Place
Greenwich, CT 06830
U.S.A.

ISBN 0-8119-0556-X

Printed in Hong Kong

Page 1: The Silver Lady, or Spirit of Ecstacy, proud mascot borne by
nearly all Rolls-Royce motorcars since 1911.
Page 2 and 3: The Camargue is the most expensive Rolls-Royce in
regular production, and one of the most costly cars in the world. The
body was styled by Pininfarina, but is built by Motor panels of Coventry.
Below: 1921 Springfield Silver Ghost sedanca de ville. Coachwork by
Brewster.

Contents

Above: The second Royce car, after it had passed into the hands of W T Glover, photographed by the Manchester Ship Canal.
Top: Lamps and screen of a 1911 Silver Ghost Roi-des-Belges tourer.

A fateful meeting

On 27 August 1877 a son was born to Lord and Lady Llangattock at their town house on Hill Street, off Berkeley Square in London's fashionable Mayfair. Within a short time telegrams of congratulations began to arrive, and among the hundreds of boys employed to deliver telegrams in those pre-telephone days was an intelligent and ambitious 14-year old named Frederick Henry Royce. The chances that this boy delivered telegrams to Hill Street are remote, but not impossible, for we know that he worked from a post office in the Mayfair district. He would not have known the telegrams' contents, and if he had it would have meant nothing to him, but the name of the new baby was Charles Stewart Rolls. It was to be nearly 27 years before the two were to meet, and to begin the partnership which was to give rise to The Best Car in the World, and set such a standard of excellence that any other company may claim that they make the Rolls-Royce of kitchen appliances, garden tools or mousetraps.

Frederick Henry Royce, known to his family as Henry, was born 27 March 1863 at Alwalton in Lincolnshire, where his father James owned a flour mill. The business did not prosper and when the boy was four years old his father took him and his elder brother to London. He found no more success there, and young Henry was sent out to earn his living at the age of nine. This was not so unusual as it might seem today, and was the lot of countless boys and girls whose parents could not afford to keep them at home, let alone pay for schooling. Henry's first job was selling newspapers for W H Smith at Clapham Junction and then Billingsgate, which occupied him until he was 11 years old. By then his father had died, and his mother somehow managed to secure about 12 month's schooling for him, after which he went to work again, this time delivering telegrams.

Early in 1878 the generosity of an aunt enabled him to take up an apprenticeship at the locomotive works of the Great Northern Railway at Peterborough, and here his mechanical education began. By day he worked on Stirling's '8-footer' engines and the evenings were spent in the little workshop at the back of the house in which he had lodgings. Guided by his landlord, a Mr Yarrow, he learned fitting and filing, and how to use a lathe. Mr Yarrow's son, who was also an apprentice at the locomotive works, recalled in later years, 'He was a very quiet lad at that time, and rarely went out at night. You couldn't keep him away from books. Although he had had hardly any schooling, he managed to teach himself quite a lot about electricity and algebra, and something also about foreign languages. I believe he had a book about French, and he studied that with the others. But electricity was the thing that interested him most.' And it was electricity that provided him with a career and, eventually, a successful business of his own. The apprenticeship came to an end after three years, because his aunt could no longer afford the £20 annual premium. The 17-year old boy set out to look for work with a glowing reference from the superintendent of the railway works, but this was of little help in the harsh climate of 1881, when one of the many slumps in the engineering industry was putting on the streets hundreds of men with more experience than Royce.

However one advantage of youth over experience is that employers could pay very little, and Royce eventually found a job with a firm of toolmakers who had a contract with the Italian Arsenal. Here he worked a 54-hour week for a basic pay of 11 shillings (55p). Overtime brought in a little more but involved working from 6.00am to 10.00pm, and sometimes all Friday night. After a year or so he was able to give up this uncongenial work and obtain a job in London with the Electrical Light & Power Company. Gaining experience by day, and attending lectures in the evenings, he soon felt able to call himself 'electrician,' and before long he was sent by his company to a subsidiary, the Lancashire Maxim & Western Electric Company in Liverpool where one of his jobs seems to have been to keep the lights functioning in the city's theaters and music halls. This was a complex task at a time when a decrease in load caused the dynamos to run too fast and transmit so many volts to the remaining lights that they burned out. Royce was now first electrician, and would send a small boy around to the theaters from time to time to see that all was well.

Unfortunately all was not well with the Lancashire Maxim & Western Electric Company, and after about 18 months it went into liquidation. By now Royce was tired of working for other people, and as he had saved £20 he went into partnership with a friend, Ernest Claremont, who had £50 to put into the venture. They rented a small workshop on Cooke Street, Hulme, Manchester, described by Royce's biographer Sir Max Pemberton as ' . . . a sorry den when the young men rented it,' though it was greatly extended and improved over the years, and was to see the birth of all Rolls-Royce cars up to 1908, including the great Silver Ghost. They called themselves Royce & Company, despite the fact that Claremont was the major shareholder, and began by subcontracting for larger concerns, making electric filaments and lamp holders. Soon they turned to the manufacture of electric bell sets, which were becoming fashionable even in quite modest homes. The Royce set consisted of a pushbutton for the door post, a trembler bell and a quantity of cotton-covered wire. The battery had to be supplied by the customer. At a price of 1/6 (7½p) each, the bell sets sold very well, and though the profit on each one was small, successful sales enabled the partners to think about expansion into other fields.

In 1891 they began to manufacture Royce's new 'sparkless' drum-wound dynamo which soon found wide acceptance, particularly in coal mining and flour milling, where the sparks from the old-fashioned dynamos were a constant danger. These brought a modest degree of prosperity to the factory, the workforce was increased, and in 1894 a company was formed under the name, Royce Limited, Electrical & Mechanical Engineers and Manufacturers of Dynamos, Motors and Kindred Articles. At about this time they were able to add the royal coat-of-arms and the words 'Contractors to HM Government' to their letterheads, though it is not certain how this privilege was earned. In 1893 both Royce and Claremont married, their brides being sisters, Minnie and Alice Punt from London. The Royces set up home at Knutsford in Cheshire, where soon afterwards Royce brought his mother to live, and where she died in 1904.

Not much is known about their home life, but there was clearly little of it because Royce was still working up to 20 hours a day on improving his products and developing new ones, and he would frequently sleep at the factory. His only interest at home was gardening, and since he was seldom home before dark he fixed an electric bulb to the end of a bamboo cane and walked around the garden with it, planting it in the ground whenever he needed to pause, and trying not to get the long flex hopelessly wound around the rose bushes. He approved of gardening, as it was a useful and productive recreation, but tennis and riding he considered criminal wastes of time. The Royces had no children, and after a while they spent less and less time together; certainly by the time of his first serious illness in 1911 he had virtually resumed the life of a bachelor.

Soon after the formation of the public company in 1894 they added electric cranes to their range of products. At that

time all heavy lifting jobs in mines, quarries, factories and building sites were performed by cumbersome steam cranes, and the lighter jobs were done by manually-operated pulleys or hand-cranked cranes. There was plenty of demand for Royce's electric cranes and hoists, and these were soon made in various sizes up to really large cranes for dockside work. Henry Royce was particularly interested in safety, and took out the first patent to limit the downward speed of a crane. This was necessary in steelworks where there had been some terrible accidents due to spillage of molten steel from crucibles. All Royce cranes had their own make of roller bearings since he could not obtain these elsewhere.

In 1893 a young man named John de Looze joined the company as cashier and book-keeper. When they went public the following year he became Secretary, and remained with Royce, and subsequently Rolls-Royce, in this post until 1943. Orders were growing rapidly, from £6000 in October 1897 to £20,000 in February 1899. In the latter year the share capital was increased to £30,000, mainly for the purpose of building additional premises, and the company seemed to have a very bright future. However, rival firms entered the electric crane market, and the continental and American products undercut the Royce cranes in price and, inevitably, quality. Royce was never one to compromise on quality, and he propounded then the maxim which lasted well into the motorcar days: 'The quality remains after the price is forgotten.' While the company was not faced with immediate disaster, the time seemed ripe for expansion into yet another field, though none of the directors were certain of what this should be.

It is unsurprising that a man of Royce's mechanical interests should buy himself an automobile as soon as they became available. His first was a de Dion-engined quadricycle, a tricycle with an extra wheel at the front, and sometimes a wickerwork passenger seat between the front wheels.

Above: Sir Henry Royce, in later life, photographed at his home at West Wittering, Sussex.

Right: A 10hp two-cylinder Decauville, of the type owned by Henry Royce in 1903. The absence of a licence plate indicates that the photo was taken before January 1, 1904.

They were crude devices at best, and it is not surprising that Royce did not keep his for long. His first proper car was a French-made Decauville which he bought in the early part of 1903. It was a conventional light car with a 10hp vertical-twin engine, four-speed gearbox, jointed drive shaft and live axle, that is, one driven through bevel gearing and not by chains or belts as many cars of that time were. Royce soon found himself dissatisfied with it, complaining of the 'terrible unreliability, noisiness and bad design.' The more he examined the car the more convinced he became that he could make something much better himself. It was not that the Decauville was a poorer car than most others of its day, for they all suffered from vibration and mechanical clatter, especially when standing still, but to Royce's purist mind these had to be eliminated. After he had worked on the Decauville until he felt there were no more improvements to be made, he announced that he would build a car of his own. There was no question at first of this being a new line of business for Royce & Co Ltd, so 'Pa' Royce, as he was already being called, installed himself in a corner of the works, appropriated two of the most promising apprentices, Tom Haldenby and Eric Platford, and set to work.

The first three cars, which were the only ones to bear the single name Royce, owed much to the Decauville in general layout. Like it, they had vertical twin engines, but Royce chose a two-throw crankshaft which gave a better balanced engine, something he would have learned to value from his railway days. The drawback of this layout is that it gives an odd exhaust sound, roughly speaking 'Bang-Bang-Silence-Silence,' whereas in engines where the crank throws are in line and the two pistons rising and falling together, the sequences is 'Bang-Silence-Bang-Silence.' However he overcame this by fitting an enormous muffler which greatly reduced the exhaust sound. He also made a much simpler and less tortuous inlet pipe system, and on the third car employed his own design of trembler coil ignition and carburetor. Careful attention to the fit and finish of all moving parts and to the tooth formation in the gearbox were other contributions to the remarkable smoothness and silence of the little Royce cars, the first of which emerged onto Cooke Street on 1 April 1904, to the accompaniment of hammering on bench, anvil or floor by all the employees.

Only grudging approval had been given to the automobile project by Royce's fellow directors and by the foremen who resented workmen being taken off the money-earning electrical jobs to help with Mr Royce's eccentric project in the corner. He was totally dedicated to his car, and worked alongside the apprentices all the time. One of them recalled that when Royce wanted a leather washer or gasket and could find nothing suitable handy, 'he tore off one of his leather leggings and threw it at me, telling me to make it out of that quickly.' He sometimes came to the works with only one legging on, or without a tie. The first drive was to Knutsford and back, with Platford and Haldenby following behind in the Decauville. Their services were not needed, however, and the run was completed without a hitch. The first test runs were made with a bare chassis, but within a week it was sent to a local coachbuilder to have a two-seat body fitted. The two other cars soon followed, these having four-seat bodies of the type known as a rear-entrance tonneau, in which the passengers entered through a small door at the back, the seats being on either side of the entrance. Of the three cars, the first was retained by Royce himself, the second went naturally to his partner Ernest Claremont, and the third, the only one to be sold, was purchased by Henry Edmunds, who had become a director of the company in 1903.

Among Edmunds' many business interests was a directorship in the Parsons Non-Skid Tyre Company, which entered a car in the 'Sideslip Trials' held by the Automobile Club of Great Britain & Ireland (today the Royal Automobile Club) in April 1904. In those days skidding, or 'the dreaded sideslip' as it was generally called, was a major problem, and the study of tire tread patterns and other ingenious devices to reduce the danger was just beginning. The Automobile Club received 16 entries for its first trials which consisted of a 1000-mile road section including braking tests followed by a course consisting of a 50-foot stretch of asphalt generously coated with Thames mud and soft soap. The Parsons company were searching for a car to borrow, and Edmunds decided to approach Henry Royce, with the result that the first Royce car was taking part in a competitive event little more than two weeks after it had emerged from the factory. Edmunds was the driver, accompanied by the official observer H Massac Buist, and reporters from various newspapers who took turns riding in the car each day. The Royce came through the trials well, and the Parsons Non-Skid device, which consisted of chains wrapped around the tires in the manner of modern snow chains, was awarded second prize.

What is highly interesting, in the light of subsequent events, is that one of the organizing committee for the trials was the Hon Charles Rolls who is almost certain to have seen the Royce car at some time during the three weeks trials. This means that his first sight of the car with which his name was to become associated took place about two weeks before his first meeting with Henry Royce, rather than immediately afterwards as has generally been assumed. This meeting was arranged by Edmunds who realized that while Royce had built an excellent little car, his lack of contacts in the motor trade would prevent him from selling it widely. Contacts were exactly what Charles Rolls possessed in abundance, so Edmunds set about bringing the two men together, not the easiest of tasks but one which he felt to be of the highest importance.

Charles Stewart Rolls was the third son of Baron Llangattock, a wealthy landowner of English descent living in Wales, where he had a property of some 6000 acres near Monmouth. Charles was educated at Eton and Trinity College, Cambridge, where he read engineering. In 1896, when he was 19, he bought a 3½hp Peugeot, the first car to be seen in the university city, and that Christmas he drove it the 180 miles from London to his Monmouthshire home. A less adventurous soul would have left the car in London for the vacation, or put it on a train, but Rolls rightly thought that cars were for driving, and though the journey took him two days including many hours spent working on it by the roadside, he arrived in time for the family's Christmas celebrations.

By the time he left Cambridge he was one of the most experienced and skilled motorists in the country. In 1899 he began his racing career, driving a Panhard in the Paris-Ostend and Paris-Boulogne races, finishing second in the tourist class in the former event, and fifth overall in the latter. The following year he won a special gold medal in the Automobile Club's 1000 Mile Trial, also in his Panhard, and in 1901 he drove a Mors into 18th place in the gruelling Paris-Berlin Race, the leading motor race of the year. By now he was well-known in motoring circles and also in London Society, and did as much as anyone after King Edward VII to introduce one group to the other. He had no need to earn a living but he couldn't spend all his time at the wheel of a racing car, so in 1902 his father set him up in business as a seller of imported cars with offices at 28 Brook Street in the heart of Mayfair, and a repair shop and garage at Lillie Hall, Seagrave Road in Fulham, just adjoining West Brompton Station. The telegraphic address for Brook Street was 'Rollicking, London,' and that for Lillie Hall 'Sideslip, London.'

He began by selling the two French makes that he knew best, Panhard and Mors, later adding the Belgian Minerva and French Gardner-Serpollet steam cars to his stable. He even dabbled with commercial vehicles for a while, offering a Swiss-built chassis for trucks and buses under the name Rolls, but few, if any, of these were sold. The cars were all expensive, selling to much the same customers who bought Rolls-Royces a few years later, and the business benefited greatly from Rolls' contacts in the drawing rooms of Mayfair and Belgravia.

Today members of the aristocracy are involved in many businesses such as photography, interior decoration, boutiques and restaurants, but in 1902 this was virtually unknown, and Rolls must have been the only 'Hon' to sell motorcars or anything else. (However, in March of that year *The Car Illustrated* magazine was started by the Hon John Scott-Montagu who was to succeed to the title of Lord Montagu of Beaulieu in 1905 and to have considerable involvement with Rolls-Royce in later years.) The business was strengthened in 1903 when Rolls took as a partner Claude Goodman Johnson, formerly Secretary of the Automobile Club and organizer of the 1000 Miles Trial.

The fact that there were no British cars in Rolls' showroom was not due to any want of patriotism, but simply because the fledgling British motor industry made few cars of the necessary quality, and those few, such as Lanchester and Napier, were already adequately represented. However, by the spring of 1904 the Panhard was not selling as well as

Above left: F H Royce & Co Ltd business paper from the early 1890s.

Right: Charles Rolls on the way up the mountain road from Ramsey, during the 1906 Tourist Trophy race. Leaning out of the car is his mechanic, Eric Platford.

formerly, having lost its pre-eminence as a pioneer make, and Rolls was looking for a new source of stock for Lillie Hall and Brook Street. When Henry Edmunds told him that there was a Manchester-built car called a Royce which was worth looking at he was not impressed at first because it had only two cylinders, and Rolls' customers were used to four. However he agreed to accompany Edmunds to Manchester (Henry Royce claimed to be far too busy to make the journey to London), and on 4 May they traveled up on the 8:30 from Euston. Edmunds later recalled that during the journey Rolls said that it was his ambition to have a car connected with his name so that it might be a household word, in the way that Steinway was with pianos, or Chubb with safes. He was only to live another six years, but his ambition was well on the way to being realized by the time of his death in 1910.

The meeting between the two men, with Edmunds no doubt acting as host, took place over lunch in the Grill Room of the Midland Hotel in Manchester, and afterwards Rolls had a short drive in what was presumably the second Royce car, as the first was still in London awaiting the final tests in the Sideslip Trials. Whatever doubts he may have had about two-cylinder engines were allayed within a few miles, for here was a twin smoother and quieter than many fours. Furthermore Henry Royce had mentioned over lunch that he did not propose to stick to twins indefinitely, but hoped to make cars with three, four and even six cylinders, if he could find the right outlet for them. Rolls returned to London already more than half decided that he had found his quality British car to sell, even if he did not yet think that it would make him a household name. A test run soon convinced Claude Johnson as well, and by August 1904 a draft agreement had been worked out by which C S Rolls & Company would take the entire output of Royce Ltd. It was not until the final signing of the agreement on 3 December that it was decided that the cars should be sold under the name Rolls-Royce, while the two companies remained separate until March 1906 when the public company, Rolls-Royce Ltd, was formed. This, in fact, replaced C S Rolls & Company, for Royce Ltd remained as a maker of electrical equipment until 1933.

During the latter half of 1904 Henry Royce was busy with the design of the first Rolls-Royce car, a 10hp twin, not greatly different from the Royce. He redesigned the crankshaft and improved the external finish, but the engine size and chassis dimensions remained the same. The most important external difference was that the rather undistinguished flat-topped radiator of the Royce was replaced by a Grecian design not unlike the Parthenon in proportions, which has been carried by every Rolls-Royce car since then. It has been suggested that the design for this came from an obscure car called the Norfolk which had just gone out of production at Cleckheaton, Yorkshire, with some of the redundant employees being taken on by Henry Royce. However this can never be proved, and the resemblance between the two designs is not all that great. What is certain is that the Rolls-Royce radiator was closely copied by many other car makers once the marque became established, notably Sizaire-Berwick in England, Secqueville-Hoyau in France, and Moon, Kenworthy and Roamer in America.

The first public showing of the 10hp Rolls-Royce was at the Paris Salon in December 1904, and a batch of 20 was begun. In fact no more than 16 were made, the last leaving the works in 1906, as the larger cars proved more popular, and as we know Charles Rolls felt that two-cylinder cars did not entirely fit in with his up-market image. The show cars were a chassis and a complete car with four-seat body by the London coachbuilders Cann & Company. Like most small cars

Above: The classic Grecian style radiator, introduced in 1904 and essentially unchanged up to the present day. No other car radiator has such a long history of continuous unaltered design. Above right: First used in 1905, the entwined R R letters are seen here on the hubcap of a current Camargue. Top right: The dashboard clock fitted to the 1911 Silver Ghost, and, bottom right: Variously known as the Flying Lady, Silver Lady, or more properly, Spirit of Ecstasy, the famous Rolls-Royce mascot was designed by the sculptor Charles Sykes, and is thought to have been inspired by Lord Montagu's secretary Eleanor Thornton.

of the period this had no doors to the rear seats, but one of the front seats could be swung sideways to afford access to the rear; this was a better system than the rear-entrance seating compartment, in which the passengers had to climb in through a little door in the back of the body, standing in the muddy road before they did so.

As well as the 10hp two-cylinder cars, there was a 20hp four-cylinder car, a 15hp three-cylinder chassis without engine, and a six-cylinder 30hp engine. All these models were advertised in *The Autocar* on 17 December 1904, and a month later C S Rolls & Company issued their first catalog. This listed four models, 10, 15, 20 and 30hp, with a variety of bodies all of which were to be supplied by Barker. Founded in 1710, this was the leading British coachbuilder of the day, and they were to supply many of the finest bodies on Rolls-Royce chassis up to 1938. Two interesting points about this first catalog of January 1905 are that for the first time the entwined R-R letters were used, and a new address appeared, 14–15 Conduit Street, Regent Street, London, premises which the company still occupy today. The Brook Street premises were retained as a branch office and showroom, as was the garage at Lillie Hall.

The issue of an optimistic catalog is one thing, but getting cars into the hands of customers is quite another, as many firms apart from C S Rolls & Company have discovered. Writing several years later, Rolls said of Royce 'I won't say he has suited me in quantity for we could have sold double or treble the number, and I see no chance of getting satisfaction in this respect for a considerable time to come.' The trouble was that Royce was wisely reluctant to turn over too much of his manufacturing resources to automobiles, and he was equally reluctant to turn out cars which had not been adequately tested. A four-model program was ambitious for a

newcomer, though manufacture was simplified by using the same cylinder dimensions for the 10, 20 and 30hp models. As the cylinders were cast in pairs, the 20hp four was made up of two twins, and the 30hp six of three. The only odd one out was the 15hp three-cylinder, which had separately cast cylinders, and the additional complications which this arrangement caused probably led to the abandonment of the model, rather than any inherent defects, as has sometimes been stated. The first three-cylinder model did not reach private hands until the late summer of 1905, after the others had begun to appear on the roads, and production was suspended before the end of the year, after only six cars had been made. Most of the production of 1905 must have been devoted to the 10 and 20hp models, and even so can barely have exceeded 50 cars. The appearance of a 30hp in the hands of Charles Rolls at Filey in June of that year occasioned comment in *The Autocar*, so there cannot have been many around.

Of all the original Rolls-Royce models, the Twenty was the most successful, and it was this model which Rolls decided to enter in the Tourist Trophy Race (TT) held on the Isle of Man in September 1905. The suggestion is said to have come from Arthur Briggs, a wealthy Yorkshire businessman who was a leading shareholder in the company, but it cannot have met with much opposition from Rolls, who was known as one of the 'four sporting Charlies' (the others were racing driver Charles Jarrott, motor dealer Charles Friswell and magazine owner Charles Cordingley) and who had been racing since 1899. The Tourist Trophy was a new event, organized by the Royal Automobile Club, and intended strictly for cars in touring trim with four-seat bodies carrying two passengers and ballast to make up the weight of the other two. The cars had to achieve a fuel consumption figure of just over 25mpg, which eliminated the really large engines but just suited the 4-liter Rolls-Royce Twenty. Two cars were prepared for the race, and they differed in several important ways from the standard Twenty. Nickel steel was used for chassis and axle forgings, which reduced the weight considerably, and a four-speed gearbox was used, in which top was a geared-up overdrive, with third being direct. This gave a slightly higher top speed (it was charmingly known as 'the sprinting gear'), but the main intention was to reduce fuel consumption. Of the two cars prepared for the race, one used a smaller bore engine (95mm) such as had been used on the very first Twenties, while the other had the standard bore of 100mm. This was because the fuel consumption figures had not been published when work on the cars began in May, and they were in fact changed at the last minute, being increased to 22.54mpg.

The cars were driven by Rolls himself and Percy Northey, and Rolls hedged his bets by entering a Minerva as well. Forty-two cars started on the 208 mile race, Rolls getting away first since he had been first to send in his application. Unfortunately, on his first lap, indeed before the first mile had been completed, he stripped the gears and came to a standstill. It seems that in order to save gasoline he was coasting downhill with the engine switched off, and in trying to re-engage the gears with a dead engine and no synchromesh he stripped the teeth off third gear. With a surprising lack of sportsmanship he suggested that the gearbox had been sabotaged, saying 'This is the sort of thing that happens frequently in France, but I hardly thought it possible that it could happen in this country.' It was left to Northey to maintain the honor

of Cooke Street, which he did very satisfactorily, finishing in first place which in fact made him second on handicap. His average speed was 33.7mph, compared with 33.9mph for the winning Arrol-Johnston.

This success was very gratifying to a small and almost brand new make of car, but its greatest importance to the company was to convince Claude Johnson that sport was a valid and indeed vital form of publicity, something he had been reluctant to accept before. In an advertisement placed in The Autocar the day after the race he claimed victory of a sort by saying that the Rolls-Royce had beaten all other cars having vertical cylinders. (The Arrol-Johnston had a horizontal engine.) In May 1906 Rolls beat the record from Monte Carlo to London by $1\frac{1}{2}$ minutes, despite losing more than three hours waiting for a boat at Boulogne. On actual running time he had gained three and a half hours over the previous record holder, Charles Jarrott, who had driven a much larger car. Further useful publicity was gained by Johnson's entry of a Thirty in the 1906 Scottish Reliability Trials. He was particularly anxious to demonstrate the superiority of the six-cylinder engine over the four, represented in this case by a

Swiss-made Martini 30/40hp car driven by its British agent Captain H H P Deasy, who later made cars under his own name. As well as the Scottish Trials, the contest involved the journey to and from Scotland, and points were awarded by RAC observers for speed, hill climbing, fuel consumption, reliability and the number of gear changes needed. Despite being beaten on sheer speed, the Rolls-Royce won the contest by 396 points.

In September 1906 Rolls again took two Twenties to the Isle of Man for the TT, the drivers being himself and Northey as before. The cars differed mainly in having Rudge-Whitworth detachable wire wheels in place of the wooden-spoked artilleries of the 1905 cars. This time fortunes were reversed, and it was Northey who went out of the race on the first lap with a broken front spring, while Rolls went on to win at an average speed of 39.3mph, nearly 4mph faster than his nearest rival, Paul Bablot in a Berliet. He was more generous in victory than he had been the previous year in defeat, and in response to a message of congratulations from *The Autocar* he replied, 'I would like to thank *The Autocar* for its congratulations, but as I had nothing to do but sit there and wait until

Queen Mary visiting a hospital at Boulogne in July 1917. Note additional headlight above the windscreen of the Silver Ghost, and the ordinary number plate. When the King and Queen traveled together their car carried no plates, a custom still observed today when the Queen is riding in an official car.

the car got to the finish, the credit is obviously due to Mr Royce the designer and builder.'

In December 1906 Rolls took one of the Tourist Trophy cars to the United States where the make was completely unknown. He entered it in a five mile race at the Empire City Track at Yonkers, NY, and won. This was followed up by demonstration runs for the American press and the exhibition of a 30hp car at the New York Motor Show. An agency was set up but it did not prosper at first.

Before passing onto the successful six-cylinder models, it is worth looking at what has been called Henry Royce's 'Brief Flirtation with Folly.' This epithet is less than kind to Royce in that the request for it came from Claude Johnson, inspired it seems by a remark of Lord Northcliffe to the effect that 'speed mania' was a thing of the past, and that what people needed was a gasoline equivalent of the electric brougham, silent and free from vibration and capable of no more than 20mph. Such gasoline-powered broughams, with their engines concealed under the driver's seat, were not unknown in 1905, but they tended to have a very high driving position, necessitated by perching the chauffeur above a vertical four-cylinder engine. This led to complicated linkages for gear-shifting with, as Anthony Bird has said, 'the hapless chauffeur receiving a sharp rap over the knuckles from the heavy brass gear lever dithering wildly on the end of its five foot stalk.' Henry Royce's response to this problem was to design an engine which would be much lower than the conventional vertical four, and what he came up with was a V-8, the first example of this layout to be designed from scratch. (There was an earlier V-8 car, made by Ader in France in 1903, but this engine consisted of two of the firm's V-4s coupled together.) This engine was located below the floor, on the passenger's side of the frame, with the steering gear and gearshift mechanism beside it, and was coupled to a three-speed gearbox and a low-geared back axle. Combined with a very flexible engine, this meant that the car was almost independent of its gearbox, and could start in high gear.

Two examples of the 'invisible engine' model were made, followed by a curious machine in which the V-8 engine was mounted in front under a very low hood, and which rejoiced in the name of 'Legalimit' as it could not exceed 20mph, the legal maximum speed at the time. This was ordered by Lord Northcliffe but he was not at all satisfied with it. His chauffeur, William Pine, recalled that on their first run from London to Sutton Place, near Guildford, they had to take three valves out and several sparkplugs. The next day Northcliffe rang up Claude Johnson and said 'The car is no damn good, Pine says so. Take it back, I don't want to spend my time on the road taking sparking plugs out!'

Later, Northcliffe developed great faith in Rolls-Royce products, so much so that he refused to believe Pine when he said that the gearbox on a Silver Ghost had 'bust'. 'What do you mean, gear has bust? Rot. You must be wrong. All right, I will phone the Rolls people.' When a man came down from Conduit Street who confirmed that second gear had gone, Northcliffe at first would not believe it.

Doubtless the problems with the V-8 engine would have been solved if Henry Royce could have devoted enough time to them, but Rolls was pressing him for increased production of the established models, and he was busy perfecting the six-cylinder engine which was by no means without faults. The market for the town brougham was a limited one anyway, and it was undoubtedly a wise decision to abandon further work on the V-8 after three cars and parts of a fourth had been made. It is the only model of Rolls-Royce of which not a single car survives to the present day.

The Silver Ghost

Right: 1913 Silver Ghost open drive limousine, chassis number 2366, with an unusual Indian-built body. owned by S M Tidy. By this time Rolls-Royce was beginning to supplant Napier as the favorite transport of the Maharajahs. Top right: A 1920 Silver Ghost armored car, chassis number 193 WO, owned by the Royal Armoured Corps. This is one of the 1920 Pattern armored cars, and is armed with a Vickers Medium Machine Gun. It saw service in Northern Ireland in 1921, Shanghai in 1927, Egypt in 1930, and was used for coastal patrol in North East England from 1940 to 1943.

When Henry Royce told Charles Rolls over that famous lunch in May 1904 that he wanted to make a car with a six-cylinder engine he was making an ambitious forecast. At that time there was only one six-cylinder car being made in Britain, the 18hp Napier, and the designers of this car faced serious problems. Chief among these was that the crankshaft was inevitably longer than in a four-cylinder engine, and being made relatively light in order to save weight it turned on its axis 'winding and unwinding like the elastic of a toy aeroplane,' as Anthony Bird said. This is an obvious exaggeration, but this twisting effect often led to broken crankshafts which caused the total destruction of the engine. The ideal solution lay in designing the crankshaft so that its natural frequency of torsional vibration lay outside the normal speed of the engine, but this is easier said than done. There is no doubt that the 30hp six-cylinder Rolls-Royce suffered from this problem, and Henry Royce soon realized that nothing short of a complete redesign of the engine would effect a cure. As we have seen, the Thirty employed three blocks of the 10hp two-cylinder engine for simplicity of manufacture, but this meant that the journals and pins designed for a twin now had to do duty for a crankshaft three times as long.

The new six-cylinder engine, which Royce was working on throughout 1906, was conceived as a brace of triplets rather than a trio of twins. It is somewhat inaccurate to think of it as simply two three-cylinder engines in line, for in fact they were back to back so that the third and fourth pistons rose and fell together. The diameters of the pins and journals were nearly twice those of the Thirty, and pressure lubrication was used in place of the splash system of the earlier engine. Royce had already tried this in the V-8. The other major redesign involved the valve layout, which was now of the L head or side valve system rather than the inlet-over-exhaust system used in the previous Rolls-Royces. The size of the engine was enlarged, giving a capacity of 7036cc compared with 6177cc for its predecessor, and the dimensions were 'square' with bore and stroke equal at 114mm (4½ inches). The power output was 48bhp, not especially high for an engine of such a size, and about the same as a 998cc Mini Metro today. The new model was originally called simply the 40hp, but very soon the designation 40/50hp was adopted.

In those days the annual automobile shows were vital shop windows for new models, and all concerned realized the importance of getting the 40/50 to London's Olympia Show which was held in November 1906. By an all-out effort two cars were prepared in time, a chassis which was shown at C S Rolls & Company's stand, and a magnificent Pullman Limousine by Barker in the Barker stand. This was said to be

Above: A Rolls-Royce Heavy Twenty tourer, photographed in France. The number plate, 1981 RR, is an early form of trade plate.
Inset, top right: The first Rolls-Royce sold in America, the 20hp TT type tourer, bought by the Texan, Captain Hutton, and seen here at Ormond Beach, Florida, in the winter of 1906.

Right: Silver Ghost enclosed drive limousine of about 1910.

a replica of one supplied to the Duke of Portland, presumably on a 30hp chassis since no 40/50s had yet been sold to the public. The Barker stand also had a landaulette on a 30hp chassis, as supplied to the Duke of Richmond and Gordon.

Production was slow to start, but 13 chassis had been turned out by April 1907, and No 13 (works chassis number 60551) was to become perhaps the most famous individual Rolls-Royce ever made. It was fitted with an open touring body by Barker to the instructions of Claude Johnson, the body being painted silver with silver plated fittings.

The car carried a plate giving its name, 'The Silver Ghost. It was quite usual at that time for cars to be given individual names, other 40/50s being called the Silent Rogue and the Dragon Fly. Although today all 40/50s made up to 1925 are commonly called Silver Ghosts (and for convenience will be so called in this book), the name was never applied generally at the time. The usual description was 40/50, although since it was the only model made from 1908 until the introduction of the Twenty in 1922, the simple description, Rolls-Royce, was perfectly adequate. It is a measure of the fame of Johnson's car, which carried the registration number AX 201,

Above: An early Silver Ghost, circa 1908, taking part in an American reliability run.

Left: One of the rare 30/40hp six-cylinder cars, made from 1905 to 1906, photographed in Cleveland, Ohio. This was not a very popular car, suffering from crankshaft vibration, and it was to replace it that Henry Royce embarked on the 40/50hp, popularly known as the Silver Ghost.

Left: A handsome Silver Ghost tourer, circa 1911, sold in America. Note the spare tires, as Rolls-Royce were not yet using detachable wheels.

that after the introduction of the Phantom I, when people wanted to make specific reference to the earlier 40/50, the name Silver Ghost immediately came to mind.

The Silver Ghost was tested by *The Autocar* in April 1907 ('At whatever speed the car is being driven on its direct third there is *no* engine as far as sensation goes, nor are one's auditory nerves troubled . . . by a fuller sound than emanates from a eight-day clock'), and the following month Johnson took it on the first of many trials in which proving and publicizing the new car were equally mixed. The first of these was a 2000 mile run observed by the Royal Automobile Club, covering the course of the forthcoming Scottish Reliability Trial, after which the car took part in the Trial itself, winning a gold medal. From Bexhill to Glasgow (about 470 miles) the lower two gears were never used; early Silver Ghosts, like the 20hp TT cars, had four speeds of which third was direct and fourth an overdrive, ideal for continuous high speed touring.

Shortly afterward the Silver Ghost was submitted to a still more searching test, being driven, almost continuously, between Glasgow and London until 15,000 miles had been covered. This was considered to be the equivalent of three years' normal use at that time. The car was then completely dismantled and examined for wear; this revealed nothing that needed urgent attention, but Johnson was such a perfectionist that he insisted on rectifying the smallest matter. The cost (in materials) of bringing the car to mint condition was £2 2s 7d (£2.12).

In 1908 the car was sold to Mr Dan Hanbury of Castle Malwood, Lyndhurst, Hampshire, who kept it until his death in 1948 when it was returned to the factory in part exchange for a modern car. Since then it has been completely restored and has appeared on the company's behalf in countless rallies, demonstrations and automobile shows. It is arguably the most valuable veteran car in existence, yet it is not stored in a museum. The total mileage must be in the region of 575,000.

During the months that these tests were taking place, no Silver Ghosts were sold to the public, whose appetite was whetted by the press accounts of the wonderful new car.

Johnson's main purpose in delaying the marketing of the car was to ensure that there were no embarrassing breakdowns when in the hands of owners, as so often happened to rivals' cars, but the increase in public interest was a valuable spin-off from his caution. Production of Ghosts began in September 1907, and soon four chassis per week were leaving the factory. The smaller two- and four-cylinder models were quietly dropped, although the decision to concentrate on a one-model policy was not made until March 1908. It was an unusual step at that time, when most of Rolls-Royce's rivals such as Napier, Fiat and Mercedes made a wide range of cars including quite cheap 'popular' models. The decision was prompted by Johnson's confidence in the Silver Ghost, and also doubtless by the move to a new and larger factory at Derby. To transfer tooling for the older models to new premises would have been unprofitable, and none of the partners showed any interest in developing new designs for smaller cars.

The move to Derby was dictated by the need for increased car production which Cooke Street could not possibly cope with, for Henry Royce was not willing to abandon the electrical work on which he had built his fame, no matter how much demand there might be for the cars. There was no special reason for choosing Derby for the new factory, but the combination of an inexpensive plot of land and a cheap supply of electricity was the final deciding factor. The new premises were much larger, covering some 12½ acres, while Cooke Street, even after enlargements, was only 3 acres. To acquire the land and build the new factory required a lot of extra capital, and in December 1906 a public issue of preferred and ordinary shares was made. The money subscribed was insufficient, but the day was saved by Arthur Briggs who wrote a check for £10,000, receiving, not surprisingly, a seat on the board for his generosity. From the prospectus issued at this time we learn that Henry Royce, as Chief Engineer and Works Director, received £1250 per year and 4½ percent of the profits in excess of £10,000, Charles Rolls and Claude Johnson £750 plus 4 percent, Ernest Claremont £250 and 2½ percent.

The Derby factory was officially opened on 9 July 1908, the electric current being switched on by Lord Montagu of Beaulieu, whose success with his magazine *The Car Illustrated* had made him much in demand for ceremonies such as this. He had also opened the extravagantly palatial Argyll works at Alexandria-by-Glasgow in 1906, but this venture went bankrupt eight years later. Better fortune attended the Rolls-Royce works which has remained with the company ever since, although today it is airplane engines and not cars which are made there.

Production at Derby was increased to about seven chassis per week, and remained at this level until the outbreak of war in August 1914. There were few major changes in the Silver Ghost's design during its life, two occurring in 1909. The engine capacity was increased from 7036 to 7428cc, raising power output from 48 to 60bhp, and the four-speed gearbox was replaced by a three-speed one. This may seem to have been a step backwards, but it was brought about as much as anything by the ignorance of the motoring public who hated gearshifting and were always enquiring how flexible a car was in high gear. Although the Silver Ghost's overdrive high gear was ideal for cruising on the level, it was not as flexible for low-speed work as the direct third. The customer would ask 'Will the Rolls climb a 14-degree hill in high gear as the Napier does?' and it was in vain that the salesman pointed out that the Rolls' third was equivalent to the Napier's high gear.

So the overdrive was abandoned, and a three-speed box with direct drive in third substituted. Four speeds returned in 1913, but this time a lower first gear was added, and high was still direct. This change came about because a Silver Ghost taking part in the 1912 Austrian Alpine Trial disgraced itself by failing to start on a 14-degree hill until the passengers dismounted. The other major change came toward the end of the car's life, in 1923, when four-wheel brakes were introduced. Royce would gladly have taken this step earlier, but there was still considerable prejudice against four-wheel brakes which were considered dangerous and more likely to promote skidding than those which operated on the rear wheels only.

It was in 1911 that Rolls-Royce cars first carried the now world-famous mascot, the Flying Lady, or more correctly, Spirit of Ecstasy. This was designed and sculpted by Charles

Above: A 1909 Silver Ghost two seater in Pennsylvania.
Above right: A 1910 Silver Ghost with unusual all-enclosed Pullman limousine body by Mulliner. This car was owned by the Hanbury family of Castle Malwood, Lyndhurst, Hampshire, and was a stablemate of the original Silver Ghost, AX 201. Next to the car is the family chauffeur, Ernest Smith.

Right: A 1911 Silver Ghost tourer with American licence plates. Note the curious pointed fronts to the fenders.

Sykes, a well-known artist, at the request of the company. Sykes was a friend of Lord Montagu, and it is believed that he introduced the artist to Claude Johnson. The model for the Flying Lady is thought to have been Eleanor Thornton who was Lord Montagu's personal assistant and who had previously worked for Johnson.

In 1910 and 1911 two serious blows befell the firm: the death of Charles Rolls was perhaps the less serious in that he had played a decreasing role in the company's affairs after the introduction of the Silver Ghost. Aviation now claimed his attention, at first ballooning and then airplanes, and in April 1910 he resigned from the post of technical managing director, becoming merely technical adviser. Three months later, on 12 July, his Wright biplane crashed during a flying meeting at Bournemouth and he was killed almost instantly.

The following year Henry Royce collapsed with severe intestinal trouble, brought about by the overwork which dated back to his teens, and total neglect of his diet even when he could afford the best. The story is often told of how his progress around the Cooke Street works was followed by apprentices carrying glasses of milk which they would endeavor to persuade him to drink, while his food consisted of chunks of bread and eggs boiled on the furnace. His biographers have always been rather coy about the exact nature of his illness but it seems as likely as not that it was ulcerative colitis, a disease often associated with stress, and one for which there was little hope of cure in Edwardian days. It is not surprising, therefore, that his doctors gave him only three months to live, but after an enforced convalescence in Norfolk he was well enough to return to the factory.

Here Claude Johnson stepped in with one of the most valuable decisions he ever made, both for his company and his friend. He realized that if Royce returned to his old way of life the doctors' forecasts would undoubtedly come true, so he took him on a lengthy tour of France during the summer and autumn of 1911, followed by a winter in Egypt. Johnson hurried back to the factory from time to time but Royce remained abroad. His marriage was virtually at an end, and although he and Minnie never divorced, they saw practically nothing of each other after his first illness.

Top left: A 1911 London-Edinburgh Silver Ghost, showing remarkably low lines for the period.
Below: A 1911 Silver Ghost tulip back limousine, chassis number 1543, coachwork by Joseph Lawton. Owned by Victor Crabb. The exposed position of the driver makes an interesting contrast with the all-enclosed bodywork of the Mulliner bodied limousine of the same date on page 22. Lawtons were a Liverpool firm who began making motor bodies in 1901, and built their first on a Rolls-Royce in 1908. Later they moved to London and were renamed Lawton-Goodman Ltd.

After the Egyptian trip, which Royce does not seem to have enjoyed very much, he and Johnson went to the French Riviera where Johnson had a villa at the little village of Le Canadel. Here Royce announced that he would like to build a house, and Johnson arranged for a plot of land to be bought. 'We can begin to build whenever you like,' he said. During the following summer, while the Villa Mimosa, as it was to be called, was being built, Royce returned to England, though not to Derby. He took a house at Crowborough in Sussex and worked on a Silver Ghost with a long stroke engine which gave greatly increased acceleration, according to his biographer Sir Max Pemberton, who rode in it. It was, however, noisier. 'It gets away much quicker, and is faster' said Royce, 'but the duchesses, perhaps, won't have it. They would call it a racing car, and you know what that means . . .' He knew that the duchess trade was vital to his company, and the long stroke engine was not pursued, although some of its points cropped up in the design of the Phantom I, 13 years later.

In December 1912 Royce was back at Le Canadel, awaiting the completion of the Villa Mimosa, when he was again taken desperately ill and had to be returned to London for an emergency operation. This left him a semi-invalid, and he required the presence of a nurse for the rest of his life. It has been suggested that he had developed cancer of the bowel, but it is just as likely that it was a recurrence of the ulcerative colitis, both of which afflictions can necessitate removal of part of the bowel and a subsequent colostomy. His nurse was Miss Ethel Aubin whom he had first met during his previous convalescence at Overstrand, and she was to remain with him for the rest of his life. There is no doubt that Claude Johnson and Ethel Aubin between them saved Henry Royce,

Right: The ideal car for the Grand Tour. A 1914 Silver Ghost photographed outside the Hotel Hungaria in Budapest, in the early 1920s.

Below: In contrast to the London-Edinburgh, here is an Alpine Eagle, higher but no less handsome. This is one of the 1913 Austrian Alpine Trials team cars, with the distinctive water tower above the radiator (right).

for while he never returned to Derby he kept in constant touch from Le Canadel and the house he later bought at West Wittering, Sussex, and remained very much *le patron* up to his death in 1933.

Despite all these personal dramas the Silver Ghost had been gradually maturing, and took on a considerably different appearance between 1907 and 1912. In company with most other cars, the concept of a more or less carriage-like body with a small hood in front was being replaced by an integral design, with a continuous line from the radiator to the rear of the bodywork. To accomplish this the radiator and hood were raised and open cars in particular took on an appearance which remained essentially unchanged until the end of the 1920s. A great variety of bodywork was done on the pre-war Silver Ghost, from simple open two-seat roadsters to limousines and landaulettes, the epitome of the duchess trade. Charles Rolls had a two-seater with engine modified to give 70bhp which he used for transporting his balloon.

Probably the most attractive to modern eyes are the open four-seat tourers of London-Edinburgh or Continental type. The former was developed from a car specially built for an RAC-observed run from London to Edinburgh in high gear. This was in response to a challenge from Napier whose energetic sponsor S F Edge had entered a 65hp six-cylinder car. The Silver Ghost has a raised compression ratio and larger carburetor and a lightweight four-seat body with no roof, but was otherwise a standard car. On fuel consumption it easily beat the Napier with a figure of 24.32 compared with 19.35mph, and in a timed run at Brooklands it again was the victor with a speed of 78.26mph to the Napier's 76.42mph. In 1912 the chassis was fitted with a streamlined single-seat body and a higher-geared rear axle, and achieved 101.8mph over the flying quarter mile at Brooklands. The driver was Ernest Hives who was to become chief

engineer of the company in later years and to receive a peerage for his work on aircraft engines. From 1912 onwards, a limited number of chassis of London-Edinburgh type were supplied to the public alongside the standard models.

The Austrian Alpine Trials were held annually from 1910 to 1914 and consisted of a searching four-day trial covering more than 1000 miles of mountain roads for cars with open four-seat bodies. In 1912 James Radley, a friend of Charles Rolls, entered his London-Edinburgh type car and was doing well until, on a 14-degree hill on the Katschberg Pass the car was stopped and failed to restart until the passengers got out and pushed. Radley lost so many marks from this incident that he retired shortly afterward, but his chagrin was nothing to that at Derby where they were simply not accustomed to disgraces of this kind. The Silver Ghost had started on steeper inclines in Scotland, but they had not allowed for the more rarified atmosphere of the Austrian Alps. The result was a lower first gear for all 1913 model Silver Ghosts, and an official entry of three cars for the 1913 Trial, as well as a private entry for Radley. As well as the four-speed gearbox, the new cars had larger radiators, an expansion chamber above the radiator cap and an extra gas tank. The engine was developed to produce about 70bhp, with a raised compression ratio and a larger choke carburetor.

All these improvements paid off, and the Rolls-Royce cars dominated the event, one winning the Archduke Leopold Cup and the others taking six awards. They missed getting the team prize only because one car had the misfortune to be rammed by a non-competing car, though even here triumph emerged from disaster, for the driver, Sinclair, managed to finish with only third gear operating. After this reassertion of their excellence, Rolls-Royce saw no need to enter again in the Alpine Trial, though Radley again ran privately in 1914 and was the only competitor to finish without loss of marks. Replicas of the team cars were marketed under the name Continental, though apparently Hives always referred to them as Alpine Eagles, and this name is often used for them today.

The years from the introduction of the Silver Ghost to the outbreak of war in 1914 were the most vital for the company in establishing its reputation. For all their qualities of silent running, the original 10 and 20hp Rolls-Royces were relatively little-known among the large number of cars on the market (about 600 different makes worldwide in 1905); from 1907 to about 1912 the Silver Ghost would have to share the honors for the title, 'Britain's Best Car' (the slogan 'The Best Car in the World' was first used by the *Pall Mall Gazette* in November 1911, and only much later in Rolls-Royce advertising) among several other makes, of which Daimler, Lanchester and Napier were the best known, but thereafter it gained ground while its rivals retreated or fell completely by the wayside. It is difficult to pinpoint the reasons for its success, but they must lie in a combination of the excellence of the car which Henry Royce produced and the skill and persistence of Claude Johnson in selling it.

The qualities of Royce were not those of an innovator, which was probably a good thing, for the byways of motoring history are littered with radical designs which failed to sell. Where he excelled was in attention to detail; he would not use chain drive for any of the engine ancillaries; instead, the gears he employed were cut to finer accuracy and by more skilled men than in any other factory. Until his breakdown in health in 1911 he would constantly prowl round the factory, and any workman handling a tool clumsily was liable to instant dismissal. Inexperience he would forgive, but never slovenliness or incompetence. The result was a car which ran more silently and gave less trouble than its rivals. It was also remarkably easy to drive. The sports car has been defined as one which rewards good driving and punishes bad driving to a greater extent than the ordinary car. The Silver Ghost, which never set out to be a sports car, rewarded the skilled, but was remarkably forgiving toward the inept driver. There were more of the latter in 1908 than today, for there were no driving tests, and all those over 35 had come to adulthood before there were any automobiles at all. Many Rolls-Royces were chauffeur driven, and the chauffeur was often a former coachman whose skills were confined to encouraging recalcitrant horses.

The First World War did not have such an immediate impact on the automobile industry as did the Second, and a number of car makers were still supplying new cars to the public two years after the outbreak of hostilities. It has been said that Rolls-Royce immediately offered the 100 or so chassis that were on hand to the War Office in August 1914, but 10 months later *The Autocar* was describing a new Alpine Eagle with a Hamshaw sporting four-seat body that had just been delivered to a civilian customer. Nevertheless the Silver Ghost was widely used by the armed forces, in three main roles, as a staff car, as a supply vehicle for armored cars with a light truck body, and as an armored car. As a staff car it was favored by most of the 'top brass' including Sir John French, Lord Kitchener and Earl Haig, while for visits to the Western Front King George V and Queen Mary abandoned the Daimlers they habitually rode in at home for Silver Ghost limousines. Rolls-Royces were also used by King's Messengers for carrying important documents to British Embassies abroad.

The supply vehicles had rather crude truck bodies, nominally for 15cwt loads though they often carried much more, and usually twin rear wheels. The first armored car was built for the RNAS (Royal Naval Air Service) which was operating ten cars and ten trucks from Dunkirk in September 1914. The main task of the cars was for patrols to supplement air reconnaissance and to rescue the crews of aircraft shot down. They were vulnerable to attack by German cavalry, and so two cars, a 45/50hp Mercedes and a Silver Ghost, were fitted experimentally with boiler plate armor by the Forges et Chantiers de France shipyard at Dunkirk. Later in September the first Rolls-Royces with armor fitted in Britain came out to France, and were known as the Admiralty pattern to distinguish them from the RNAS pattern armored in Dunkirk. Early Admiralty pattern cars had open bodies with armor over the radiator, body sides and rear, and 'spats' over the front wheels, but these were soon replaced by the turreted pattern which had much better protection for the crew in an enclosed turret, but dispensed with the spats which must have added to the weight and proved very awkward in mud. The standard armament was a Vickers-Maxim machine gun.

The Rolls-Royce was the most widely used of all British armored cars in the First World War, and saw service in France, Egypt, Palestine, Arabia and East Africa. Apart from flat tires, inevitable when carrying twice the load they were designed for over extremely rough roads in intense heat, they gave practically no trouble, and earned the deep respect of many who had never encountered a Rolls-Royce in peacetime. Colonel T E Lawrence used armored cars and supply vehicles in his campaigns and attributed much of his success to the speed and maneuverability of the cars. 'A Rolls in the desert was above rubies,' he said later. Normally speeds were restricted to 20mph to conserve tires, but if necessary a Rolls armored car could exceed 50mph. The author's father learned to drive in Egypt on a Silver Ghost supply vehicle and

a D-type Vauxhall touring car on which he and young fellow officers took turns driving around an improvized course marked out with beer bottles and oil drums in the desert, only one of the group having ever handled a car beforehand.

After the war a new pattern of Rolls-Royce armored car was made, generally similar to the 1914 Admiralty pattern but distinguishable by its disk wheels in place of wire ones. These saw service in Ireland, Afghanistan and India; some of them, and the later 1924 models, were still in use at the

Above: A Rolls-Royce armored car and a Daimler ambulance of the Guards Division, collecting wounded soldiers near Guillemont on the Western Front, September 14th, 1916. The armored car is the Admiralty Turreted Pattern.

Right: 1925 Silver Ghost tourer, chassis number 120 EU, coachwork by Barker. Owned by John Hampton. This was the last Silver Ghost to be delivered (June 3 1925) and went to a London jeweller who preferred it to the newly introduced Phantom 1.

outbreak of World War 2. Most were used for training in Britain, but the 11th Hussars in Egypt had some fitted with a Boys anti-tank rifle and Bren light machine gun. These were used in action in the early Libyan campaign in 1940–41.

The Silver Ghost was quickly put back in production after the Armistice, and the postwar model was described in the press in April 1919. Engine, gearbox and chassis were unchanged from 1914, but the new car had electric lights and a self-starter which had only been fitted as extras before the war. The new generators and starter motors were of Rolls-Royce's own make. The price of a chassis was £1450, compared with £985 in 1914, but so great was the car hunger of the time that a secondhand 1914 model which had cost £1145 complete sold for £3000 in 1919. Many fortunes had been made in the war and there was no shortage of money for luxury cars in the first two or three years of peace.

This brought forth a number of new designs to compete with Rolls-Royce, including the straight-eight Leyland from a firm which had previously made only trucks and buses, the V-8 Guy from another commercial vehicle concern, and the British Ensign with six-cylinder overhead-cam engine. None of these was made in large numbers, but a more serious rival was the new H6 Hispano-Suiza from France, whose $6\frac{1}{2}$-liter overhead-cam engine developed 135bhp compared with 75 to 80bhp for the post-war Ghost, and which had four-wheel power brakes. It was more expensive than the Ghost and not as silent, but it had the attraction of being rare on British roads and distinctly exotic, part of the fashionable, slightly raffish world of post-war Mayfair and Monte Carlo. It was almost inevitable that Iris March, the rich, doomed heroine of Michael Arlen's *The Green Hat*, should have driven a Hispano, while it also featured in a French novel very popular on both sides of the Channel, *l'Homme à l'Hispano* by Pierre Frondaie. If it was much too flashy for the duchess trade, there were those duchesses and others of the *ancien régime* who thought that the Rolls-Royce was too obviously a rich man's car, especially as it had become almost regulation wear for those who had made a quick fortune during the war. The war profiteer was an unloved figure, much caricatured in the press and criticized on the stage, and the phrase 'too profiteery' was readily used for any form of ostentation.

There is no doubt that Rolls-Royce caught some of the backwash of these feelings, and there are still old chauffeurs around who will tell you that 'the real people' preferred Daimlers. Nevertheless Henry Royce was not one to let rivals hold an advantage for too long, and in 1923 it was announced that next year's models would have four-wheel power brakes of the Hispano's pattern. Although they were not standardized until well into 1924 they could be installed at the company's expense to all cars ordered after November 1923. Other changes were being planned, including an overhead valve engine, but these justified a change of name, which came with the introduction in May 1925 of the New Phantom, or Phantom I as it has been called.

Main picture: 1929 Phantom 11, chassis number 124 WJ, coachwork by Kellner. Owned by Nick Whitaker. This car was first owned by Sir Pomeroy Burton who sent the chassis to Kellner in Paris to have the body, known in France as a Coupé Chauffeur, made to his order. Inset: 1974 Phantom VI limousine, coachwork by H J Mulliner/Park Ward, owned by Douglas Bunn. This is the flagship of the current Rolls-Royce range, and is made in very limited numbers, currently not more than 12 to 15 cars per year.

The Phantoms

In May 1925 the long-awaited replacement for the Silver Ghost was announced, under the name New Phantom. Its current name of Phantom I was used only after the introduction four years later of the Phantom II. At first the company said that it did not supersede the Silver Ghost, but supplemented it, presumably to allay the fears of any purchasers who wanted to stick with the old model with which they were familiar. One customer, John Henry Thomas, Chairman of Tardery Thomas, the London costume jewelers, had ordered a Silver Ghost in December 1924, and since the New Phantom was introduced before his car was complete, was offered the new engine instead. However, he had had such good service from his 1909 Silver Ghost with which he had covered 307,000 miles that he declined the offer, and his car which was completed with its Barker bodywork on 3 June 1925 was the last Silver Ghost. The chassis was built for armored car bodywork as late as 1928.

The main differences between the New Phantom and its predecessors lay in the engine which had a detachable cylinder head and pushrod-operated overhead valves as in the Twenty. The capacity was larger, at 7668cc, this being obtained by using a considerably longer stroke ($5\frac{1}{2}$ inches compared with $4\frac{3}{4}$ inches). The cylinder bore was in fact smaller at $4\frac{1}{4}$ inches instead of $4\frac{1}{2}$, and this resulted in a lower horsepower rating (43.3 instead of 48.6) and consequently a lower annual tax, £44 compared with £49. As on the Twenty there were hand-controlled radiator vents, but vertical rather than horizontal. The chassis was virtually identical to that of the last Silver Ghosts, with spiral bevel final drive which had been introduced on the Ghost in 1923. The most important improvement during the New Phantom's short lifetime was the replacement of the cast-iron cylinder head by an aluminum one in 1928. The company had already begun their policy of not disclosing power outputs, but the new engine probably developed 90bhp in its original form, and something over 100bhp by the last models of 1929. It was in many ways an interim model between the well-tried Silver Ghost and the much more modern Phantom II which was to take the company into the 1930s, and is one of the least favored of Rolls-Royces among present-day collectors. It lacks the lightness of feel that distinguished the prewar Silver Ghosts, and the steering tends to be heavy because of the balloon tires which were coming into fashion at the time of its introduction. However this was a fault of all large cars at this time, and the New Phantom was still pleasant to drive compared with a contemporary Daimler, Napier or Panhard.

Right: 1927 Phantom 1 limousine, chassis number 76 RF, coachwork by Erdmann & Rossi, owned by Klaus Riebold. This is believed to be the oldest surviving body by the famous Berlin coachbuilders on a Rolls-Royce chassis. Erdmann & Rossi were the leading German firm to build bodies on R-R and Bentley chassis, and made at least sixty between about 1926 anmd 1939.

Below left and below: 1927 Phantom 1 sedanca-de-ville, chassis number 76 TC, coachwork by Clark of Wolverhampton. Owned by Stanley Sears. This car was commissioned by C W Gasque, a director of Woolworths, for his wife. The Louis XIV interior includes genuine Aubusson petit point upholstery, and hand painted door panels and ceiling. The upholstery alone took nine months to make, and cost £600.

Above: 1929 Phantom 1 tourer, chassis number LF 75, coachwork by Barker, owned by C D Ellis. One of the last Phantom 1s made, this car was originally owned by the Maharajah of Baroda.
Top: 1928 Phantom 1 saloon, chassis number 91 EH, coachwork by Hooper. Owned by Roger Bunn. Known as the Black Diamond, this car was built for the diamond merchant Otto Oppenheimer, and had a secret compartment for carrying the gems. Accessories and radiator are silver plated.

Top: 1929 Phantom 1 sedana -de-ville, chassis number 74 OR, coachwork by Barker, owned by R Pennington. Founded in 1710, Barker were the senior British coachbuilders up to their liquidation in 1938. Although mainly traditional they were responsible for several new developments, including the Barker headlight dipper and wheel disk.

Before the New Phantom was many months old, one with a relatively light touring car body was taken to Brooklands for speed tests. To the chagrin of all concerned its maximum was only 74mph, which did not compare very well with the 78.5mph achieved by a London-Edinburgh Silver Ghost in 1911. Of course speed was not of primary interest to most Rolls-Royce customers, but the younger engineers

were nettled by the decline in performance over 14 years, and Claude Johnson, though he was now 62 years old, was anxious to have a faster car, not as the sole model, but as an alternative to offer to the more sporting customer who was buying Bentleys and Sunbeams. He therefore authorized the building of a special Phantom with light sports body by Barker, chassis number 10 EX. This was still not much faster than the standard model, largely because of the weight of the body. Ivan Evernden, who was particularly responsible for liaison between the company and the bodymakers, had a difficult time persuading Barkers to build a body with flared fenders and a pointed tail, so different from their normal trade. However they did, and the result was a car which achieved 89.11mph over the flying half mile.

Three other experimental cars with sports bodywork generally similar to that of 10 EX were built, the 15 EX, with Hooper body, the 16 EX (Barker) and the 17 EX (Jarvis). There was never a production sports Phantom I because the 17 EX was not completed until the autumn of 1928, by which date work on the Phantom II was under way. 10 EX was nicknamed the Claude Johnson Special, but he saw little of its development as he died in April 1926 after a short illness, aged only 63. Doubtless his ceaseless efforts to protect the health of Henry Royce had sapped his own, as well as the

Above left: 1931 Phantom II sports saloon, chassis number 9 GX, coachwork by Barker, owned by Paget L W Bellin. A very attractive looking car, and ideal for long distance touring.

long hours of work that he put in during the war. The debt that the company owed to him is incalculable, for it is unlikely that Rolls-Royce would have survived had it not been for his wise administration, and the restraining hand he placed on Henry Royce's quest for perfection. Left to himself, Royce would have pursued the ideal of the perfect automobile beyond the limits of commercial common sense, and the company would quite possibly have foundered. The involvement of the company in aircraft engines was also initially Johnson's, although once he had been pushed in that direction, Royce worked with tremendous enthusiasm.

One of Johnson's lesser-known ideas was the formation of the school for chauffeurs, and the system of regular inspection of owners' cars. He first concerned himself with the chauffeur question when he visited a Mr Barclay in Herefordshire in 1908 to find out how he was getting on with his two-year-old 30hp Rolls-Royce. He found that the chauffeur kept the car in good condition, but that his driving left a great deal to be desired. 'He drives, in my opinion, far too fast round blind corners and is likely to have a bad smash, but as a criticism of driver's methods (apart from his care of the mechanism of the car) appears to cast a reflection on the owner's sanity, I refrained from making any remarks, but devoutly thanked my Maker when I alighted from the car.'

The immediate consequence of this visit was Johnson's decision to offer ten cash prizes of £25 each to the ten chauffeurs who, in the opinion of the Directors, had kept their cars in the best condition during the previous 12 months. This was later changed to a Certificate of Merit and cash gifts to all Rolls-Royce chauffeurs who satisfied the inspectors over a period of at least two years. These inspectors were very august persons in the eyes of chauffeurs, and would come down from London in chauffeur-driven cars to make their investigations. The inspection took all day, and was infinitely more searching than the present British Ministry of Transport test, according to one chauffeur. If they were satisfied they would recommend a cash reward, but would not actually make it until they had received the agreement of the employer. If dissatisfied, they would never give their reasons.

The School of Instruction, or Drivers' Demonstration Class, as it was called at first, was launched in October 1910, and was set up for beginners with little or no experience with cars, and for experienced drivers. Even the latter were expected to attend for at least six days, while for beginners three or four weeks was considered necessary. Drivers were told that they were not to ramble about the works at leisure. 'Rolls-Royce Limited have found that their workmen are very easily dis-

Below: 1930 Phantom II all-weather tourer, chassis number 49 GY, coachwork by T H Gill, owned by Victor Crabb.

turbed by the presence of strangers, and discipline is thereby seriously affected.'

The course remained at Derby until the mid-1920s, when the New Phantom was being tested. Naturally rumors of this car reached the ears of chauffeurs on the course, and they reported back to their employers that the Silver Ghost was to be replaced, thus hurting sales. Johnson therefore ruled that the course must be taken away from Derby so that no one outside the company would know what was going on, and in 1925 the school was moved to Seleng House, Ewell, Surrey. Here it remained until 1930 when it moved to Cricklewood, then to Colindale, and finally to the Rolls-Royce Service Depot at Hythe Road, Willesden, where it is located today. Accommodation is no longer provided, but at Seleng House pupils could be lodged on the premises, and the list of rules make amusing reading today. Among them were the following:

No intoxicating liquor whatever is to be brought into the house.

Gambling or playing for money is prohibited.

Pupils are not allowed in the kitchen.

Please remember that there are other houses nearby, the inhabitants of which may object to unnecessary noise etc. The house is closed each night at *11 o'clock* and all pupils must be in by that time.

All lights out at *11.30 pm.*

From the earliest days of the school, Rolls-Royce stressed that the course was for Rolls-Royce chauffeurs and owners of the cars, and there had always been a sprinkling of the latter among the pupils. It is not unknown for American enthusiasts to include the course as part of a vacation trip to London. In the 1930s tuition was granted in special cases to pupils who were not Rolls-Royce owners or in the employ of such owners, but in this case the fee for the twelve-day course was £10, compared with the regular fee of £7. Today it is over £100 for a ten-day course.

The basic features of the courses have changed little over the years, as a comparison between brochures for the early 1930s and the present day shows. Then, with a greater variety of models, the classes were divided into four distinct sections, for the following cars:

(1) the 40/50hp Phantom II
(2) the 40/50hp New Phantom (now known as Phantom I)
(3) the 40/50 Silver Ghost
(4) the 20/25hp car

Each classroom contained a set of sectioned units of the particular chassis. A week's instruction filled about 35 pages of notes in an exercise book. It is interesting that the company thought it worthwhile having a section for the Silver Ghost which had been superseded some eight years earlier, but there were still a large number on the road. Today there is but one course, as all Rolls-Royces have the same engine, but individual points of Silver Spirit, Corniche, Camargue and Phantom VI are pointed out as they arise. The course is approximately 70 percent classroom instruction and 30 percent on the road, though the latter will include a certain amount of maneuvering tests on the premises. One of the tests in pre-war days involved placing a full glass of water on the radiator, then starting the engine, driving a short

Left: 1934 Phantom II drophead coupe, chassis number 175 RY, coachwork by H J Mulliner, owned by Frank Dale. Mulliner also built this very attractive style on the 20/25 chassis.

Below: 1933 Phantom II Continental sports saloon, chassis number 104 MY, coachwork by Hooper, owned by D S Crowther.

distance and braking gently to a halt. The trainees had to pay for broken glasses.

Nearly 7000 people have passed through the School since it began. There is nothing else like it in the world today, though the Daimler company operated a course from 1929 to 1939, and Napier gave cash awards to chauffeurs with several years good service.

In September 1929 the New Phantom was replaced by the Phantom II, again not a completely new car but very different in appearance from its predecessor. This time the major changes were in the chassis, while the engine remained substantially the same as in the Phantom I. The frame was much lower, and semi-elliptic springs were used all around in place of having cantilevers at the rear. The car had a much lower look, even with formal limousine bodywork, and in the opinion of many people the Phantom II was the best looking Rolls-Royce ever built. The engine, clutch housing and gearbox were now assembled as one unit, and a chassis advance borrowed from the American Rolls-Royce factory in Springfield, Massachusetts was central lubrication, being operated by a pedal from the driving compartment. It was not yet a one-shot system, for it did not extend to the kingpins and other movable joints on the axles, which were dealt with by an oil gun. However it was a vast improvement on the Silver Ghost which needed, if the chauffeur or owner were properly conscientious, 99 points lubricated by hand once a week. On later Phantom IIs even the kingpins were covered by the centralized system, through the use of flexible tubing. Improvements to the engine included a redesign of the combustion chambers and manifolds with inlet and exhaust now on opposite sides of the engine. The capacity was the same but power output went up to about 120bhp.

As with other prewar Rolls-Royces, a great variety of bodies was fitted to the Phantom II, including many formal limousines demanded by the 'rich old lady' customers. However, it was available in two wheelbase lengths, the regular one of 150 inches and the 'short' of 144 inches, and it was on the latter that were built most of the Continental models. These had their origin in a prototype, chassis number 26 EX, on which was mounted a four-seat sports saloon body built by Barker but designed by Ivan Evernden in close cooperation with Henry Royce. On Royce's instructions, Evernden had bought a Riley Nine Monaco sedan and the two men worked to produce a body in the spirit of the Riley but of course scaled up to suit the Phantom II chassis. The spare tires were removed from their usual place on the side of the hood to the rear, and the fenders were flared, exposing their undersides, a feature of a number of the hairier sports cars of the 1920s and also used by Evernden on the 'sports' Phantom I prototypes.

It was fitted with a sunshine roof, and finished in a pale saxe-blue color with a coat of artificial pearl lacquer over it. This coating was produced by mixing clear lacquer with finely ground herring scales. A color scheme such as this was quite a novelty for a Rolls-Royce, most of which tended to be finished in somber black or dark blue. In September 1930 Evernden took the car on a Continental tour, and, making a last-minute entry in a Concours d'Elegance at Biarritz, walked off with the Grand Prix d'Honneur. This resulted in a satisfying number of orders from France and Spain for the new car, even before a catalog had been produced. By the time Evernden returned home he found that the publicity department had indeed produced a brochure featuring photos of the car taken at the Biarritz Concours.

The second prototype Continental, 27 EX, had a generally similar body made by Park Ward. This company, which alone of all the great British bodymakers survives today (amalgamated with H J Mulliner), was little known in 1930, and came to Henry Royce's notice when he saw a Park Ward-bodied car outside the Conduit Street showrooms. Attracted by the lightness of construction and better visibility than most cars of the day, he told Evernden to visit Park Ward's Willesden premises the next day, and this began an association between the two companies which lasted until 1939 when Park Ward was bought up by Rolls-Royce. By 1932 Park Ward were supplying 'recommended' bodies on the Phantom II chassis as well as on the 20/25. The former included a long-wheelbase seven-passenger limousine and a short-wheelbase Continental sports sedan. The Continental was

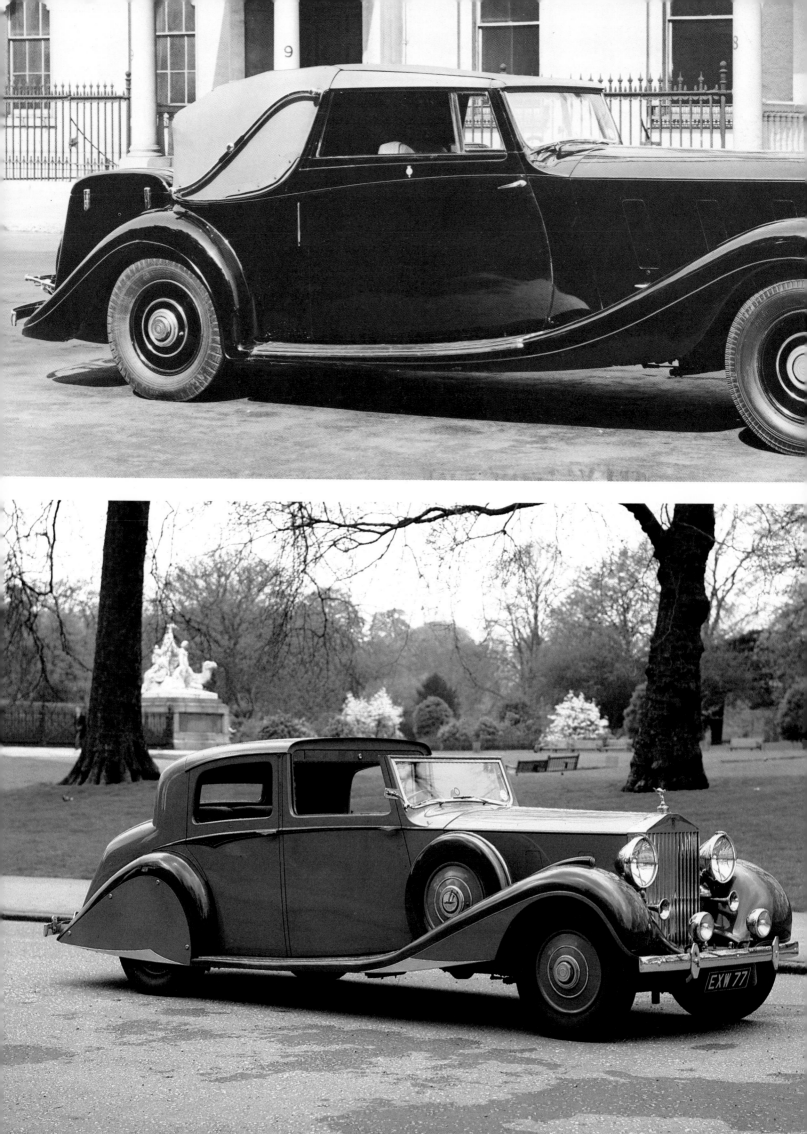

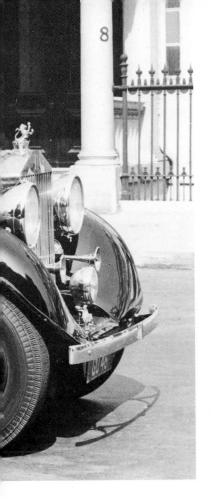

Left: a 1936 Phantom III, chassis number 3AZ 158, with drop-head coupe body by Gurney Nutting. The King of Rumania had an almost identical car, apart from hood louvers and a chromium strip on the waist line.

Bottom left: 1937 Phantom III sedanca-de-ville, chassis number 3CP 200, coachwork by Hooper. More flamboyant than most Hooper bodies, this one was in fact styled by the French *carrossier* Saoutchik of Paris, and built by Hooper in London. It is unusual in that the steel roof panel can be slid back, making the rear portion of the car into a convertible.

never strictly defined by the makers, and a great many statements have been made about the attributes of a genuine Continental. According to the American expert, Raymond Gentile, who has made a study of the model, the only two factors that determine and permit the title Continental chassis are a wheelbase length of 144 inches, and flattened front springs, five in number, in place of nine thinner leaves used on the regular Phantom IIs. Other factors, such as the lower rake of the steering column, were fitted to most, but not all Continentals, while some so-called Continentals with the longer 150 inch wheelbase do not, in Mr Gentile's opinion, qualify. A total of 281 genuine Continentals was made, out of 1681 Phantom IIs in all.

The main improvements in the Phantom II were synchromesh on the two top gears in 1933 and on second gear as well in 1935, and shock absorbers controllable from the steering column introduced in 1933. A higher compression engine came in 1933, giving a short-chassis Continental a top speed of around 95mph.

The Phantom II was the last design of Henry Royce, for on 22 April 1933 the great man died. He had been largely bedridden for the previous six months, although his interest in the firm and in new designs had never abated, and he had a design team constantly working with him at his Sussex home at West Wittering. In 1930 he had been made a baronet for his work on the aircraft engines which had won the Schneider Trophy for Britain. Despite his being a semi-invalid, he had survived all the original team of his own generation with the exception of company secretary John de Looze who lived until 1953. Johnson had been dead for seven years and Rolls for nearly 23 years, his original partner Ernest Claremont died in the early 1920s (though his brother attended Royce's cremation), and Henry Edmunds died in 1927. Amid the gloom it is pleasant to note that the faithful nurse Ethel Aubin married Royce's solicitor not long after her employer's death. Royce's ashes remained in the Number 1 shop at the Derby works until 1939.

The engineering department was now under the control of A G Elliott and Ernest Hives, who was more concerned with aircraft engines in the 1930s. Hives finished up as Chairman of the company and a Companion of Honor. The managing director was Arthur Sidgreaves who had taken over from Claude Johnson's brother Basil, and the Chairman up to 1944 was Lord Herbert Scott. Even before Royce died, consideration was being given to a replacement for the Phantom II, and it had been decided that this should have more than six cylinders, because to extract greater power from a six-cylinder unit and retain the traditional Rolls-Royce smoothness and silence would not have been possible. A straight eight might have been a possibility, but the layout which appealed more was the V-12. Rolls-Royce already had plenty of experience with aircraft engines of this layout, and it had been adopted by Daimler in 1927, and by several American companies such as Cadillac, Lincoln and Packard. So it was a V-12 that Elliott and his team worked on from 1932, and the first prototype began its road trials early in 1934.

At first it was planned to replace the traditional flat, upright radiator with a new design with a V shape sloping toward the bottom, but Evernden was so much against it that the plan was dropped, and whatever changes there may be in the proportion of the radiator, it is unlikely that the traditional design will ever now be altered. Not only did the Spectre have a brand new engine but it also featured independent front suspension of a new design, though one which had already been used by General Motors in the United States. So many problems arose that early in 1935 it was by no means ready for production, and an exasperated Sidgreaves, anxious for a new model, asked if they could not use the Spectre engine in a Phantom II chassis, which would result in a car as 'new' as the Phantom I had been when compared with the Silver Ghost. However work at Derby and testing on the Continent proceeded feverishly, and the new car was ready to be introduced to the public in October 1935 at the London Motor Show, under the name Phantom III. No fewer than nine cars were exhibited, either on the Rolls-Royce stand or those of various bodymakers, but only one, chassis No 37 EX on the Park Ward stand, had an engine, the others being dummies. This did not keep people from ordering the new model, though, and in fact even before full details had been announced, several customers who had Phantom IIs on order canceled them in favor of the new model.

The V-12 engine had pushrod-operated overhead valves with a capacity of 7340cc developing about 165bhp in the original models, and 180bhp by 1938. The four-speed gearbox, with synchromesh on the three upper forward speeds, was not made in a unit with the engine as the Phantom IIs had been, but was mounted further back in the chassis. This apparently backward step was taken so that the weight of the gearbox would compensate for that of the engine, which had been shifted forward a little, and also to reduce the length of the drive shaft. The more forward mounting of engine and radiator made a significant difference in the appearance of the car compared with its predecessor, and the classical perfection of the Phantom II's lines was lost. Many Phantom IIIs are very handsome cars, but they have an air of opulence rather than understatement. Alas, on subsequent Rolls-Royces the radiator was moved still further forward in the interests of maximizing the accommodation on a relatively short wheelbase, but as this has happened with every other make of car as well, one cannot single out Rolls-Royce for criticism. The independent suspension of the front wheels was a modified form of the General Motors system, with coil springs operating in oil-filled tubular boxes.

In retrospect the Phantom III has a mixed reputation. It was undoubtedly the most complex design made by Rolls-Royce, and one that requires expert and conscientious attention if the engine is not to present problems. The item that is most often quoted in criticism of the Phantom III is that of the hydraulic tappets, or more correctly hydraulic rams that kept the tappet clearances automatically correct. These required clinically clean oil if they were to function properly, and this meant that the oil filters had to be taken out and washed with gasoline every few hundred miles. Human nature being what it is, this was not always done regularly, and the Phantom III got a reputation for trouble with its tappets and was compared unfavorably with the less complex Phantom II. The result was that the company would convert the tappets to solid ones if requested, and from 1938 the hydraulic tappets were abandoned.

The other, more general, reason for the model's bad reputation is that after the war they gradually passed into the hand of less wealthy owners who did not employ chauffeurs and did not maintain the cars as their complexity demanded. Then when they went wrong, the overhaul was far more costly than on almost any other car, and this has led many Rolls-Royce enthusiasts to avoid the Phantom III. Their long hibernation during World War 2 didn't help, particularly if they were badly prepared for storage and then too hastily put back on the road. One chauffeur described the steps by which he cleaned out the petrol tank of a Phantom III laid up for six years as follows:

(1) three applications of neat caustic soda
(2) three applications of paraffin and water
(3) one application of paraffin and oil
(4) flush out with water
(5) mop out with flannel on a stiff wire
(6) fill with petrol

After this the car started first time.

Because of damaged or troublesome engines a number of Phantom IIIs were re-engined with the straight-eight Rolls-Royce unit made for the Phantom IV, which is at least less of a sacrilege than the Bedford truck engines with which some Daimlers were powered.

A total of 710 Phantom IIIs were made, and as can be imagined they were fitted with the finest bodywork of the day, both British and foreign. They were exported to 22 countries, of which the United States took the most (35), followed by France (27) and India (19). The company took careful note of individual requirements, and from the order books one may glean many comments such as the following:

chassis 3-AZ-66 Hooper sports limousine. Special attention to springs. Customer does not want harsh springing.
chassis 3-AZ-106 Park Ward limousine. UK & Continental touring at comparatively high speed.
chassis 3-CM-57 Hooper sports limousine. Car for use in UK and on the Continent. Normally used by two persons at speeds of 50–55mph, but for six weeks at much higher speeds on Continental roads with 4/5 passengers.
chassis 3-CM-71 Hooper limousine. Customer is a confirmed invalid. Speed only 35mph for UK, town work and touring. Special attention to springing.
chassis 3-DL-144 Binder sedanca de ville. France and Switzerland — mainly touring. Special adjustments to be made to prevent car from exceeding 120km/hour. (75mph).

A special request which involved more than the usual number of modifications was one for a wealthy Kent stockbroker who had owned a number of Packards with central gearshifts, and when he came to order a Phantom III he specified this layout as well. The result, chassis No 3-DL-94, was the only Phantom III to have a central gearshift, while he also specified 'no mascot to the radiator, two spare wheels and all the instruments to have white dials and black figures,' which was exactly the opposite of the standard arrangement on the Phantom III.

A study of the list of customers for the Phantom III indicates that the British aristocracy had overcome their disdain for the Rolls-Royce by the mid-1930s, for they include the Dukes of Devonshire and Sutherland, the Duchess of Marlborough, the Marquess of Queensberry, the Earls of Derby and Dudley, and many viscounts, barons and baronets. In fact one wonders how widespread the prejudice against the Rolls-Royce ever was, for even in the 1920s the car had several ducal customers, including the eccentric 11th Duke of Bedford who had 20 cars and 16 chauffeurs at Woburn, including at least four Rolls-Royces. The large numbers were necessary as he would never travel from the country to London with the same car and chauffeur, since he maintained that country chauffeurs could not be trusted in London traffic. The 'country crew' (he always traveled with two chauffeurs ever since the day when one broke his wrist trying to crank a 60hp Napier miles from anywhere) had to garage their car at Hendon and hand over their ducal charge to the town chauffeurs who would drive him on to Belgrave Square. The Duke was not an easy man to please; once when the Duchess gave him a Rolls Twenty as a birthday present, he knocked his head climbing into it for the first time. 'Take it away,' he commanded to the representative who was standing in attendance: 'It's too small. Supply a big one.'

Although Daimler was still the official car of the British Royal Family, several members of the family bought Rolls-Royces. The Prince of Wales ordered a Phantom I with Gurney Nutting Weymann sedan bodywork in 1928, and several times visited the bodymakers to inspect progress on his car. Both the Duke of Kent and Duke of Gloucester owned Phantom IIIs, while the former also had a 3½-liter Bentley and the latter a Wraith. Among foreign royalty, King Carol of Romania, King Farouk of Egypt and the Shah of Iran all had Phantom IIIs, as did many Indian maharajahs.

Production of the Phantom III ceased at the outbreak of war in September 1939, but several were rebodied after the war. Among these was an all-weather touring car by Hooper for King Ibn Saud of Saudi Arabia, which was completed in the summer of 1946. This had extra wide runningboards for the escorting guards, a small spotlight on the passenger's side of the windshield and a siren in matching position on the opposite side. Among the interior fittings, all provided by the Goldsmiths & Silversmiths Co Ltd, was a silver ablution set for ceremonial purposes. Unfortunately the King did not use this car very often, as he liked to sit in front, but protocol did not permit him to sit at the left hand of the chauffeur.

Among other post-war bodies were a striking razor-edge sedanca de ville by Freestone & Webb for financier John Gaul, and an extraordinary open roadster by Labourdette of Paris commissioned by a New York furrier. The chassis originally carried a Hooper sedanca de ville body, but the new body was an all-enveloping shell with concealed headlights and, most remarkable of all, a rounded radiator grille which totally disguised the make of chassis. Only the Flying Lady proclaimed that the car was a Rolls-Royce, and she was gold plated rather than the traditional silver. Very few bodymakers have ever disguised the Rolls radiator in this way, and the only other examples the author can think of were a French Binder roadster on a Phantom II which was subsequently modified to employ a traditional radiator, and the

Above: The first Phantom IV with H J Mulliner limousine bodywork, chassis number 4 AF 2, taken during a visit of Her Majesty the Queen to Salisbury. The car carries the St George and Dragon mascot in place of the Flying Lady, and as always when the Monarch is riding in it, no number plates. Now 33 years old, this car is still in use by the Royal Family. Below: 1953 Phantom IV, chassis number 4 BP 1, with Hooper limousine body, for King Faisal of Iraq.

first of Nubar Gulbenkian's Hooper-bodied Silver Wraiths of 1947.

The Phantom III marked the end of an era for Rolls-Royce, as all the postwar models were derived from the Wraith. It would not have survived long after 1939 anyway, as a replacement powered by a straight-eight engine was already being tested. Code-named Big Bertha, this was to be the larger of a two-model program; the smaller was to be a six using many of the same components and the same cylinder dimensions, a policy reminiscent of Henry Royce's 10, 20 and 30hp cars of 1905. However, in the harsher economic climate of the postwar era, only the small six survived, although a few straight-eights were made under the name Phantom IV for heads of state.

Despite the complexity and expense associated with ownership of a Phantom III, there are still many enthusiasts of the model; approximately 300 survive, with two-thirds of these being in America. Many owners would probably echo the great Rolls-Royce fancier David Scott-Moncrieff who once wrote 'I suppose if I were rich enough I should have two Phantom IIIs; one with an Owen Sedanca Coupé body in a hundred percent perfect condition for road use, and one stripped chassis, in a glass case, just to look at!'

Small is beautiful
– the 20hp models

Above: 1936 25/30 sedanca drophead coupe, chassis number GXM 5, coachwork by Salmons, owned by Lawrence Dalton and described by its owner as a pretty car rather than an elegant one. The coachbuilders, Salmons & Sons, of Newport Pagnell, were well-known between the wars for drophead bodies on a wide variety of chassis, sold under the name Tickford. Today's Aston Martin cars are made in the same factory. Top: Engine of a 1934 20/25. Made from 1929 to 1936, the 20/25 was a logical development of the Twenty, being a monobloc six-cylinder unit with detachable head and coil ignition.

By 1921 the postwar boom in luxury cars was over, for two good reasons. The good sales of 1919 and 1920 meant that most of the people in the market for expensive cars already had one, and even the most extravagant *nouveau riche* was not very likely to replace a new Rolls-Royce in under two years. Also wages and the cost of raw materials had risen sharply, and there was a prolonged molders' strike in 1921 which put an end to more than one British car manufacturer. The effect on Rolls-Royce was to raise the price of a Silver Ghost chassis from £1450 to £1850 by December 1920 and to £2250 in June 1921. Claude Johnson was worried about the impact of socialism on his rich customers, for the numbers of Labour MPs in Parliament had risen considerably, though they were not to achieve a majority until 1924, and then only a short-lived one. Everything, therefore, pointed to the need for a cheaper Rolls, and while he was planning to introduce the Silver Ghost in America he at the same time asked Henry Royce to design a small car which would sacrifice nothing in quality but would sell at around half the price of the larger car.

When the 'Baby Rolls' appeared in October 1922 it was seen to have a number of modern features compared with its larger companion, but also some which disappointed the purists. Among the former were a monobloc casting for the six-cylinder engine, overhead valves and a detachable cylinder head, while among the latter were coil and battery ignition in place of the magneto, and worst of all, a three-speed gearbox with a central stick. These were regarded as typical of the cheaper American car, and led the motoring writer J T C Moore-Brabazon, later Lord Brabazon of Tara (who had acted as Charles Rolls' mechanic in the Irish Races of 1903) to describe the newcomer as 'A very excellent vehicle of somewhat uninteresting American type.' In fact a four-speed gearbox and right hand shift were used on the Twenty from 1925 onward, and the lever remained on the right in Rolls-Royces until the introduction of automatic transmission in 1952.

The price of a chassis was £1100, to which an average touring car body added about £490. In its original form the Twenty engine developed 53bhp which, with a reasonable open body, gave a top speed of around 62mph. Unfortunately many buyers endowed their Twenties with seven-seat limousine bodies similar to those carried by Silver Ghosts, and the combination of increased weight and wind resistance brought down the performance considerably. To be fair, the average buyer of a Twenty limousine did not look for sparkling performance, and it was only when vintage car enthusiasts came to own them after World War 2 that the appellation of 'gutless wonder' was applied to the cars.

The engine of the Twenty is extremely significant in the history of Rolls-Royce, for it was progressively developed through the inter-war years and revived after World War 2 to be further developed until the company finally went over to a V-8 power unit in 1959. By this time its capacity had increased from 3127cc to 4887cc and its power output from 53 to 178bhp. Just about the only dimension to remain unchanged over 37 years was that between the center of the cylinder bores; 4.150 inches. This was chosen to give adequate space for cooling water.

In 1922 Rolls-Royce were a long way from doing their own bodywork, but when the Twenty was announced the company offered a number of standard or recommended body styles which, although built by Barker, were to the design of Ivan Evernden of Rolls-Royce. These included a

touring car, limousine and landaulette. Although they were made in limited numbers the price was quite reasonable, especially as they carried the prestige of the Barker name, still the leading one in British bodymaking at that time. The touring car cost only £490, the limousine £600 and the landaulette the same. Countless other bodymakers tried their hand on the Twenty chassis, including such foreign ones as Binder in France and Brewster in America. A number of Indian maharajahs bought richly ornate Twenties as stablemates to the Silver Ghosts and Phantoms which were their more usual transport, while one of the more unusual Twenties was that owned by Lord Lonsdale. Painted in his traditional yellow, it carried a very high landaulette body originally mounted on a 1910 Napier and transferred to the Rolls-Royce because none of the 1920s bodies allowed enough headroom for his Lordship's top hat.

The Twenty was made until 1929, and there were few changes apart from the move to a right-hand shift and a four-speed box already mentioned. Four-wheel brakes came in 1925, and the biggest change in the car's appearance took place in 1928 when the horizontal radiator vents were replaced by vertical ones, bringing its appearance more into line with the Phantom I which had always had vertical vents. These vents had been introduced to provide variable airflow to the radiator, and were later thermostatically controlled. The later Twenties were very similar in appearance to their successors, the 20/25s, which were introduced in October 1929. These had larger engines, at 3669cc, which developed 65–70bhp and could propel the cars at speeds from 66 to 76mph depending on the body. Although less glamorous than the Phantoms, the 20/25 and its successors the 25/30 and Wraith brought the satisfaction of Rolls-Royce owner-

Above: 1922 Springfield-built Silver Ghost Pall Mall tourer, chassis number 76 UG, coachwork by Rolls-Royce Custom Coachwork. This five-passenger touring car was the cheapest body style offered by the America Rolls-Royce company in 1922. The term Rolls-Royce Custom Coachwork covered designs by the company and built by a number of local firms, before the company set up its own coachbuilding department in Springfield in 1923.

Left: 1923 Twenty fabric saloon, chassis number 54 S 5, coachwork probably by H J Mulliner, owned by John Simonson. Right: 1925 Twenty coupe, chassis number GA 68, coachwork by Flewitt. Owned by M R Neale. These are two good examples of the Twenty, the so-called 'Baby Rolls' whose coil ignition and central gearchange shocked the purists, but which outsold the larger cars and was the basis of the six-cylinder Rolls-Royce engine right up to 1959.

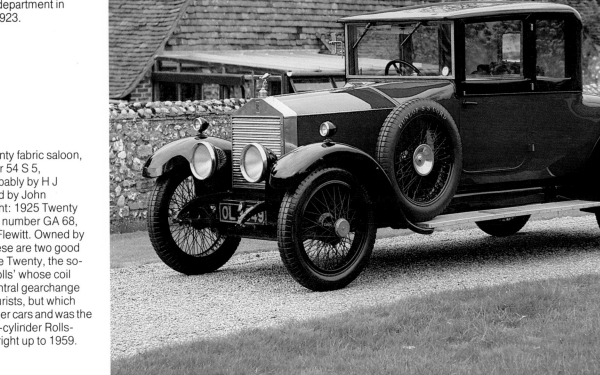

ship to a wider public, and sold in respectable numbers during the depression years of the early 1930s. While it can never be proved, it is possible that had Johnson not begun the two-model policy the company might not have survived the depression as a car maker. Without the smaller model to build their postwar program on, there would probably have been no Rolls-Royces after World War II.

The 20/25 was in turn replaced by the 25/30 in 1936 although the smaller model was still available for another 12 months or so. Again it was a question of evolution rather than any drastic changes; engine capacity went up to 4257cc and power to about 115bhp, though Rolls-Royce did not publish figures for power outputs, merely stating them to be 'adequate'. A sign of the times was the use of a number of components bought from outside suppliers which had formerly been made by Rolls themselves. These included Zenith-Stromberg carburetors, SU fuel pumps, a Bijur starter and Lucas electric equipment. The latter in particular would have been frowned on by Henry Royce, but he had been dead three years and the company had to keep a sharp eye on costs. In fact the 25/30 was a good buy at £1050 for the chassis, to which a good sports sedan body by Barker or Hooper would add about £600. The contemporary 'Big Rolls', the Phantom III, would have cost just about £1000 more than this.

The last of the prewar descendents of the Twenty was the Wraith, introduced for the 1939 season. Although the engine dimensions were the same as in the 25/30 it had larger valves and a lot of thought had gone into redesigning the crankshaft, big end bearings and engine mountings, resulting in an even quieter engine than before. The most important difference lay in the front suspension, which was now independent, by coil springs and unequal length semi-trailing wishbones. This was similar to the system which Rolls had introduced on the Phantom III three years earlier. Unfortunately production of the Wraith was halted by the outbreak of war when only 491 had been built, and it remains one of the least-known of Rolls-Royce models.

The Twenty family was the favorite basis for the building of so-called replica bodies which became quite an industry in Britain in the 1930s. Actually, replica is a misleading word, for far from being copies of something old, these bodies were up-to-date designs which were mounted on old chassis. Many a Twenty chassis of the mid-1920s had plenty of life left in it ten years later, but the styling, particularly of the enclosed models, had become hopelessly antique, and there was no vogue for vintage cars in those days. The solution was to build a new body, usually a two-door drop-head coupé, or four-door sports sedan on a chassis which had been thoroughly reconditioned and sometimes updated, and to sell the result for around £400 to £500.

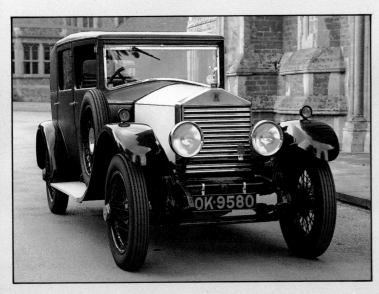

Above: Another view of John Simonson's Twenty. The body of this car is later than the chassis, and was fitted by Paddon Bros in 1939. Above right: 1933 20/25 close-coupled sports saloon, chassis number GBA 29, coachwork by Hooper, owned by Michael M O Jodrell.

Right: 1930 20/25 coupe, chassis number GDP 41, coachwork by Carlton, owned by J W Bowdage. Below: 1926 Twenty drop-head coupe, chassis number GYK 30, replica coachwork by Compton, 1931, owned by Jack Wakely.

Two firms in particular went in for this trade, Southern Motors in Clapham, South London, and Comptons of Sydenham, South East London. Neither made their own bodies, but obtained them from Ranalah and Coachcraft. These firms were by no means in the Barker league, or even the 'second division' represented by such bodymakers as Freestone & Webb or Windover, but the customer was getting what looked to the uninitiated like an up-to-date Rolls-Royce for less than a third of the price of a new one. Most of the chassis used were post-1926 Twenties for the earlier ones with rear-wheel brakes only and three-speed gearboxes were too anti-quated, and to have converted them would have been unrealistically expensive. Among regular 'improvements' were the replacement of the horizontal radiator vents by vertical ones, the fitting of smaller 19-inch wheels, a more modern steering wheel (a Comptons' specialty), and a com-plete overhaul of the engine with new pistons. The chassis were submitted to Rolls-Royce for a 24 hour test, which shows that the idea had the company's blessing. This may seem surprising, but they wouldn't have lost any sales of new cars to someone with only £500 to spend, anyway, and the fact that the cars were checked by them meant that the Rolls reputation for reliability was more likely to be upheld.

Southern Motors and Comptons' activities started in 1936, and by August 1939 they were also building replicas on 20/25 and even 25/30 chassis, though the latter is curious in that the styling of their original bodies had barely dated in

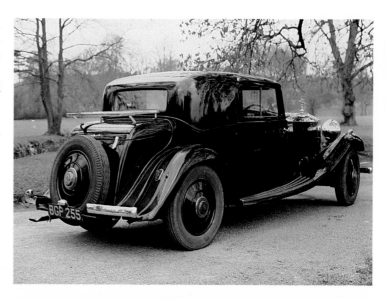

Left: 1934 20/25 fixed-head coupe, chassis number GED 17, coachwork by Freestone & Webb, owned by A W McDowell.
Center left: Coachmaker's plate for the above car. In contrast to firms like Barker and Hooper which dated back to horse carriage days, Freestone & Webb was only founded in 1923. They built about fifteen bodies a year on Rolls-Royce chassis, and stayed in business until 1958.
Right: The engine of Mr McDowell's car.

Below right: 1934 20/25 saloon, chassis number GMD 77, coachwork by Barker, owned by J E Clarke. A typical body by England's premier coachbuilder on the small Rolls-Royce chassis, this would have cost about £650, with the chassis selling for £1050.
Below left: Three-quarter view of the 20/25 Freestone & Webb coupe.

three years, while the price of a secondhand example must have meant very little profit from the £695 they were asking. Some replica bodies were built on Phantom I and II chassis, but never so many, presumably because of the horrendous thirst of the larger cars that made them attractive only to the rich who could afford new ones. Even when they were not rebodied, the Twenties were very long-lived cars. By the 1930s they were popular in the taxi trade. John Fasal, the great Twenty enthusiast, reports that in 1942 almost every taxi plying in Blackpool was a small Rolls-Royce; even three-speed models survived in Edinburgh into the early 1950s, while the author recalls riding in a Twenty limousine taxi in Canterbury as late as 1956.

Many people would argue that the greatest contribution made by the small Rolls-Royce to motoring history was that the 20/25 gave birth to the revived Bentley. In July 1931 Bentley Motors Ltd went into receivership, and not long afterward Napier put in a bid for the company. A rival to Rolls-Royce in earlier years, Napier had not made cars since 1924, preferring to concentrate on aircraft engines, but it saw an opportunity to return to four wheels and to capitalize on the Bentley reputation for high performance cars. Before the final agreement had been signed, Napier engineers and W O Bentley had begun work on the new car which was to have a $6\frac{1}{4}$-liter overhead-cam six-cylinder engine in a dropped frame. The approval of the Receiver's Court seemed a mere formality, but during the hearing a lawyer representing a hitherto unknown group called the British Central Equitable Trust offered a larger bid for the assets of Bentley.

Napier's lawyer immediately asked for a little time to gain his principals' consent to making a better offer. This was granted, but when the other barrister tried to bid higher still the judge said rather acidly that it was not his function to preside over an auction sale, and that both parties must make sealed bids. This they did, and Napier was outbid by more than £20,000. No one knew who the mysterious Trust represented, and W O Bentley himself only learned who his future employers were to be a week later when his wife returned from a party to say that she had overheard a man indicate that his company had taken over Bentley Motors. She found out the man's name from her hostess, and on her return home said to her husband, 'It was Arthur Sidgreaves. Who is he?' 'He's the managing director of Rolls-Royce,' Bentley replied.

Although he was employed by Rolls-Royce from 1931 to 1935, Bentley had no part in the design of the new car, which was the work of Ernest Hives and Roy Robotham. It was very much more than a hotted-up 20/25, for it had a new chassis which had originally been intended for an 18hp $2\frac{3}{4}$-liter Rolls

Above: 1933 20/25 saloon, chassis number GSY 44, coachwork by Wylder, owned by M J James. Note the curiously shaped front door. Wylder was a lesser known coachbuilder which flourished from 1923 to 1937.

Left and right: 1935 20/25 sedanca de ville, chassis number GBJ 22, coachwork by Fernandez et Darrin. Owned by Val Danneskold. Fernandez et Darrin was a Parisian company, although Howard Darrin was an American who designed the Kaiser-Darrin sportscar in the 1950s. This car has much more extravagant lines than most Rolls-Royce bodies; it was built for Lady Davis of Montreal.

Left: 1936 Bentley 3½-litre saloon, chassis number B 162 FB, coachwork by Park Ward, owned by S R Metcalfe. Park Ward were one of the two 'recommended' coachbuilders for the Bentley chassis, and probably built more bodies on Bentleys than any other firm.

Right: The Van Vooren-bodied 4¼-litre Bentley which covered 114.7 miles in the hour at Brooklands. It was originally registered in France, and only received its British number plate, FXW 6, in June 1939. This photograph was taken at a postwar race meeting in Britain.
Below: 1936 25/30 sports limousine, chassis number GTL 20, coachwork by Thrupp & Maberly, owned by Jack Major. This is a somewhat unusual body in that it combines the informal lines of a sports saloon with a division between chauffeur and passenger compartments, hence the name 'sports limousine'.

CYV 777

that never progressed farther than a prototype. In this was installed an engine which had the same dimensions as the 20/25 but with higher compression ratio, twin carburetors and improved cylinder head design. Power was about 105bhp compared with 85bhp for the later 20/25. Inevitably the car was a disappointment to those who worshipped the old-school Bentleys with their burbling exhausts, outside gearshifts and Bulldog Drummond image, but it was very little slower over a cross-country route, and carried modern bodywork which no one could deny was more comfortable, and most of it very handsome as well. As with Rolls-Royces, the Bentley was supplied only as a chassis, but there were a number of 'recommended' bodies, particularly by Park Ward and Vanden Plas. These were not only cheaper than genuine custom bodies, but they involved a shorter waiting time for delivery. Some handbuilt bodies could take more than six months to build, and there might well be a waiting list before work could even start.

A total of 1191 3½-liter Bentleys were made from 1933 to 1936, the final models having shock absorbers adjustable from the steering wheel. They were replaced by the 4¼-liter model which used the same engine as the Rolls 25/30 and gave about the same performance as its predecessor with the heavier coachwork which customers tended to ask for. The final prewar model was the Mark V, introduced in 1939, which had the coil independent front suspension of the Wraith and an overdrive gearbox, making the car ideal for cruising on the new motorways of Germany and Italy.

In 1938 a 4¼-liter with lightweight streamlined body by Van Vooren of Paris was ordered by the Rolls-Royce Paris manager, Walter Sleator, for a Greek customer called Embiricos. Sleator borrowed this car for several high-speed continental runs, including one on the German *Autobahnen* in which they covered five miles at 110mph, followed by four miles at 112mph. This was a remarkable performance from a car with leaf-spring suspension all round, for the *Autobahnen* were none too smooth even when new, and there was a lot of heavy traffic to contend with. This car later covered 107 miles in the hour at Montlhéry, and 114.7 miles in the hour at Brooklands. It was raced privately at Le Mans from 1949 to 1951, its best place being 6th in 1949.

Made in the USA

Above: 1931 Phantom II Newmarket convertible, chassis number 220 AJS, coachwork by Brewster, owned by Dr John A Bowers. One of the best-looking Brewster bodies on the American Rolls-Royce chassis, the Newmarket was a Phantom I style, but a few were fitted to British-built Phantom II chassis. Top left: 1925 Springfield Silver Ghost Stratford convertible coupe, chassis number S84 PM, coachwork by Brewster, owned by Dr John A Bowers. The Stratford design was built by both Rolls-Royce Custom Coachwork and by Brewster.

In September 1906 Charles Rolls paid his first visit to America on what was to be a combined sporting and sales trip. He took with him his valet, his mechanic and three cars, two 30hp and the Light 20hp that Percy Northey had driven in the Tourist Trophy race. With this car he won a five mile race at the Empire City Track against competition from much larger cars including a 45hp Peerless and 60hp Renault. The car was subsequently sold to a Captain Hutton from Texas who became the first American buyer of a Rolls-Royce car. He and Rolls' mechanic Reginald Macready campaigned the car with some success at Ormond Beach, Florida that winter before it accompanied its owner back to Texas.

The two 30hp cars were displayed at the New York Auto Show in December, one on the stand and the other being used as a demonstrator by Rolls himself. One can imagine that the merits of the car were amplified by having a real English aristocrat show them off, and Rolls certainly knew how to get the best out of the car. Three cars were sold at the show, and a fourth ordered by the newly appointed agents for Canada, Ketchum & Company of Ottawa. The American distributor was a Mr W C Martin of New York City and he ordered 17 chassis during 1907, both 30hp and Silver Ghosts.

One of the first deliveries of the year was to Mrs John Jacob Astor; she was so much the leader of New York society that it was said that if she grew tired of a performance at the Metropolitan Opera and left during the interval, everyone else left too, and the cast sang to an empty house. They didn't follow her so slavishly in the matter of automobiles, though, and Martin did not fulfil his promise to order 50 cars in 1908. They were undoubtedly expensive, at $8000 for a Silver Ghost chassis, compared with $6500 for a Lozier, $6000 for a Pierce Great Arrow and $4600 for a Thomas (complete cars in each case), all comparable American cars of the day. However money was not lacking in America then, and it seems the reason for the low sales lay in unambitious marketing and public relations.

Little was heard of Rolls-Royce in America for about six years, until 1914 in fact, when the old-established body-making firm of Brewster became the US distributors, with an efficient service backup which was organized by Claude Johnson. About 100 cars were sold up to the outbreak of war, 45 of them bodied by Brewster. Ten years later Rolls-Royce of America was to acquire Brewster whose bodymaking output was thereafter largely confined to Rolls-Royce chassis for the rest of the company's existence.

In the summer of 1919 Johnson returned to America with

Right: 1921 Springfield Silver Ghost sedanca de ville, coachwork by Brewster. This is the body style known as the Salamanca, named for Don Carlos de Salamanca, the Spanish Rolls-Royce dealer who had won the 1913 Spanish Grand Prix at the wheel of a Silver Ghost. Above: Carriage lamp on the Salamanca. This was not a standard feature. Below: 1921 Silver Ghost Albany dual-cowl phaeton.

more ambitious plans. He felt that the United States represented a more reliable market for expensive cars in the long term (there was nothing remotely resembling the Labour Party in America for one thing!) but import duties prevented a British-built car from being competitive. The answer was to set up a manufacturing plant in the US, and a factory was acquired from the American Wire Wheel Company at Springfield, Massachusetts. It was a good location since there was a ready supply of skilled labor, and Springfield was conveniently placed between New York City and Boston, which were seen as the two most important markets. British regulations forbade the transfer of funds to the United States, so the financing had to be raised locally, but this was achieved without too much difficulty, the leading backers being New York investment bankers J E Aldred and Henry J Fuller, and a wealthy Canadian, L J Belknap, who had been associated with Western Electric and had made a fortune building power stations.

Early in 1920 it was announced in the press that a limited number of Rolls-Royce chassis would be produced at the American works, that they would be identical and interchangeable with those produced at Derby, and that production operations would be under the direct supervision of trained experts from Derby. The Engineer-in-Chief of the American operations would be F Henry Royce. The 'trained experts' were represented by 53 supervisors and foremen who emigrated to Springfield with their wives and families.

No matter where they came from, the Springfield workforce developed a fierce pride in their product, and signs reading 'Let's beat Derby' were hung in every department.

The promise that the cars would be identical to the Derby products soon evaporated, though not necessarily to the detriment of the American versions. It was obvious that if a locally-made component could do the job as well as one imported 3000 miles from Britain, it made sense to use the local one. Thus the Watford magneto gave way to an American Bosch, the British generator and starter to a Bijur unit, and Dunlop wire wheels to American Buffalo wheels. An additional advantage of using American components was that they could be serviced much more readily. Production began in 1921, and only the first 25 chassis were identical to the Derby Silver Ghost. As in prewar days, and despite the absence of import duties, the price was considerably higher than that of any other American car. With an average sedan body a 1921 Springfield Silver Ghost cost $14,500, while a chassis alone was $11,750. The only other American car in five figures was the Locomobile 48 which cost $11,000 complete, while a Pierce-Arrow was $8550 and a Packard Twin Six only $6800.

The plates on the earlier Springfield cars bear the name 'Rolls-Royce Custom Coachwork' which meant that they were designed by Rolls-Royce (the bodywork drawing office was in the premises previously occupied by Knox Automobile Company, famous for air-cooled cars and pioneer articulated trucks) and built by a number of bodymakers including Smith Springfield, Merrimac of Merrimac, Massachusetts, Biddle & Smart of Amesbury, Massachusetts, and Willoughby of Utica, NY. To keep costs down, most body styles were produced in batches of 20 or more. Most of them bore very English names such as Pall Mall, Oxford, Buckingham, Canterbury, Tilbury,

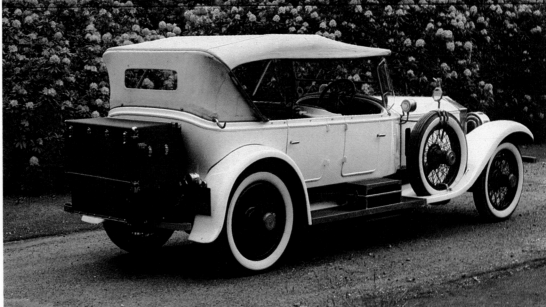

Left: A 1923 Springfield Silver Ghost with Salamanca Permanent Town Car body by Rolls-Royce Custom Coachworks. The convertible version of the Salamanca was known, perhaps rather unfortunately, as the Collapsible Town Car.
Above and top: 1922 Springfield Silver Ghost Pall Mall tourer, chassis number 76 UG, coachwork by Rolls-Royce Custom Coachwork. This term covered a number of designs which were built by local firms to the order of Rolls-Royce of America Inc.

Piccadilly and Pickwick. The only exception was the Salamanca, a town car named after Don Carlos de Salamanca, the Spanish Rolls-Royce agent who had won the 1913 Spanish Grand Prix at the wheel of a Silver Ghost. This choice of names indicates the snob appeal of anything British, but perhaps this appeal was more imagined than real, for within a few years some of the names given to Springfield Phantom I body styles were more cosmopolitan, such as Trouville, Riviera, St Regis and Newport.

In 1923 Rolls-Royce of America set up their own body-making department on Waltham Avenue in Springfield, and no longer farmed the work out, though of course there were always the special requests for bodywork from any of the major American firms such as Brunn, Derham, Locke or

Holbrook. Prices of the Springfield cars crept upward; in November 1924 the following figures were quoted, fob the Works, war tax extra:

Pall Mall	Five Passenger Touring	$12,930
Oxford	Seven passenger Touring	$13,450
Piccadilly	Roadster	$13,450
Tilbury	Enclosed Drive Cabriolet	$14,860
Windsor	Open Drive Limousine	$14,900
Pickwick	Sedan	$14,970
Canterbury	Suburban Limousine	$14,970
Carlton	Limousine Brougham	$15,200
Salamanca	Town car	$15,560
Riviera	Three-quarter Cabriolet	$15,560
Mayfair	Full Cabriolet	$15,880

These prices must be compared with contemporary cars in the US market to give a sense of proportion. A Locomobile 48, probably the most expensive domestic car, cost $7900 to $11,200, a Pierce-Arrow $7000, a Cadillac V-8 Imperial Limousine $4400, and the cheapest Ford Model T roadster $260.

The main reason for the November 1924 price increase was the changeover from right-hand to left-hand drive. The earlier Springfield Ghosts had right-hand drive not just because they were close in design to the British car, but because right-hand drive was not uncommon on expensive cars in 1921. Pierce-Arrow still featured it, and an advantage was that the chauffeur could step straight out onto the pavement to open the door for the passengers. Many high-quality European cars, and not necessarily chauffeur-driven ones, such as Lancia, Bugatti and Delahaye, employed right-hand drive up to World War 2, the explanation probably being that this was safer when driving on unfenced mountain roads. However, in America even Rolls-Royces were beginning to be driven by their owners, and with increasing city traffic they found changing lanes and passing difficult with right-hand drive.

The conversion to left-hand drive involved designing a new exhaust manifold, and altering the axle, pedal shaft, steering gear and control linkage. This was done in the factory on new cars, for existing right-hand drive cars were not converted, and in fact they became something of a sales

1925 Springfield Silver Ghost Stratford convertible coupe, chassis number S84 PM, coachwork by Brewster, owned by Dr John A Bowers. British names such as Stratford, Windsor, Newmarket, etc, were popular choices for body styles on American Rolls-Royces in the 1920s.

problem. Arthur Soutter, a senior engineer with Rolls-Royce of America, recalls that when left-hand drive became available, many older cars were traded in and were difficult to dispose of as the owner drivers who formed the biggest market for second-hand cars were just those who distrusted right-hand drive. A separate Used Car Division was established at the New York branch to deal with second-hand sales.

In 1925 the Brewster company got into financial difficulties, largely through money lost on building a complete car with a Knight sleeve-valve engine, and Rolls-Royce of America acquired control, effective from 1 January 1926. This meant that they now had the services of America's most prestigious bodymaker at their disposal, and an increasing proportion of Springfield cars were bodied by Brewster, although the Rolls-Royce Custom Coachworks continued to operate for a few years, and Brewster also built the occasional body on other chassis than Rolls-Royce. Some very handsome bodies were built by Brewster, particularly the Derby and Speedster Tourers and York Roadster on the Phantom I chassis. Other handsome and characteristically Brewster designs were the Avon sedan, the Newmarket convertible sedan and the Riviera town car. The design of these was largely the work of John S Inskip, who was later to become president of Brewster, and to play a leading part in the story of Rolls-Royce in America.

Rolls-Royce customers still went to other bodymakers, of course, and one of the most unusual cars was that built for Harry Orndorf of Providence, Rhode Island. In December 1926 he took delivery of the first Springfield Phantom I, and after five years he requested Rolls-Royce to lengthen the chassis from the stock $146\frac{1}{2}$ inch wheelbase to an enormous 160 inches. The chassis was then sent to the bodymakers Waterhouse of Webster, Massachusetts, and a very special town car body was built. The rear of the body shell was over the center line of the rear axle, which was only possible with such a long chassis, and this gave maximum riding comfort. The rear seats were duplicates of two of the owner's favorite armchairs, and the floor was covered with an Oriental rug. However the most unusual feature of the car was the two-octave chime which was built in the spare tire housing on the driver's side of the car. From a keyboard mounted on the passenger side of the dashboard, Mr Orndorff could play tunes of his choice while his chauffeur drove him along. The total cost of this conversion was said to be in the region of $30,000.

The years 1923 to 1926 were very successful for Rolls-Royce of America, and between 325 and 365 were delivered each year. Production was still not much more than one third of that at Derby, but Springfield's chairman Henry J Fuller confidently predicted that the tables would be turned; 'It is only a question of time before the US will correctly reflect the buying power of the two countries.' However he underesti-

Right and below: 1929 Phantom I sedan, originally with Park Ward fabric saloon coachwork, and rebodied by Brewster as a Huntingdon sedan.

mated the competition from other American makes, which were more numerous in the luxury field than were Derby's rivals, and the fact that Derby had an export market to Europe, South Africa and Australia, and also a smaller model in the Twenty to keep their sales figures up. And neither he nor anyone else realized that the biggest economic depression of the 20th century was only three and a half years away.

In fact, Rolls-Royce of America was in trouble before the depression struck, their problems beginning with the enormous amount of retooling necessary to change over to production of the Phantom I. Delivery of the new model was not possible at first, and to keep customers from switching to other makes, Springfield had to import more than 100 Phantom Is from Derby on which they made little, if any, profit. A lot of secrecy was necessary in the development of the Phantom I so that sales of the Silver Ghost would not fall away in anticipation of the new model. Drawings of new parts issued to outside suppliers were all stamped 'Aero & Marine Division' as a red herring, but in fact all this was in vain as the Phantom I was announced in England a full year before it was available in America, so everyone knew it was coming.

The Springfield Phantom I (or New Phantom as it was called at first) was both more and less advanced than its British counterpart. Among its innovations not adopted by Derby until later were centralized chassis lubrication operated from the dashboard, and thermostatic radiator vents, but on the debit side it did not have four-wheel brakes until early 1927. In fact these first 66 rear-braked Phantoms were subsequently recalled and updated. Prices were higher than for the Silver Ghost; in 1929 they ran from $17,840 for the Derby four-passenger touring car and York roadster to $19,965 for the Trouville town car. An aluminum cylinder head was introduced during 1929, but sales were dropping (275 in 1928, 251 in 1929) and a new and potentially very damaging problem was presented by the introduction at Derby of the Phantom II.

This was much more of a new car than the Phantom I had been compared with the Ghost, and Springfield simply could not afford the $1 million or so necessary for retooling. There was no alternative but to relinquish their manufacturing rights, but this was not quite the end of the Springfield story, for Derby agreed to make a small series of left-hand drive Phantom IIs which would be bodied in America. Delivery of these did not start until 1931, and meanwhile Springfield assembled more than 200 Phantom Is from existing stocks of components. The last of these was not delivered until 1935. The imported Phantom II chassis carried some very handsome bodywork, as befitted a model which was arguably the most attractive Rolls-Royce ever made, including the Henley roadster, Newmarket convertible sedan and Newport town car. A total of 125 lhd Phantom IIs were supplied between 1931 and 1934, of which 116 went to the US, three to Canada and six to Europe. One or two were rebodied by Darrin or Bohman & Schwartz as late as 1939, but they were not so successful aesthetically as the Brewster cars. The final fling of Brewster, which was still a subsidiary of Rolls-Royce of America, was to build town car and roadster bodies on lengthened Ford V-8 chassis; 135 of these were made in 1934 and 1935, and they were said to satisfy the needs of those who wanted Brewster craftsmanship but could not afford a Rolls-Royce, or did not want to flaunt their wealth at a time when three million of their fellow Americans were out of work, and former stockbrokers were selling apples on Fifth Avenue.

In August 1934 the name, Rolls-Royce of America, was changed to the Springfield Manufacturing Corporation, it is said under pressure from Derby who did not want the name Rolls-Royce to be associated with bankruptcy. Less than a year later the newly-named company filed a petition for bankruptcy. In 1936 the assets of the company, apart from the Springfield plant, were sold to the Pierce-Arrow Sales Company of New York, but Pierce-Arrow itself went out of business two years later. The Springfield plant was rented out to small industries while a buyer was sought; it was eventually divided into three lots and sold in 1939. The total return was $65,000 for a property that had cost $440,000.

The question is often asked whether Rolls-Royce of America could have survived had there been no depression in the 1930s. The answer is probably no, simply because of the small volume of sales, which could not justify the introduction of new models to keep pace with Derby. Apart from the fact that they were obliged by their contract with the parent company to keep pace in the matter of new models, they obviously needed to if they were to keep up with the

increasingly strong rivalry from American manufacturers. If they could not afford to retool for the Phantom II in 1929, it is unlikely that they could have done so for the V-12 Phantom III in 1935, yet Cadillac, Lincoln, Packard and Pierce-Arrow were all making excellent V-12s by this date, and Cadillac had a V-16 as well.

It is significant that the only one of these four companies to fail in the next few years was the one that had no line of cheaper cars, Pierce-Arrow. Rolls-Royce clearly had no cheaper line, for the small six-cylinder cars were quite unsuited to the American market, and anyway a 20/25 cost as much as a big Packard. However it would be unfair to say that the whole American adventure was Claude Johnson's folly; it was a successful business for a number of years, and produced some beautiful cars which gave other American manufacturers a high standard to aim at.

Many of America's most prominent families were numbered among Springfield's customers; the list of owners includes such names as Carnegie, Guggenheim, Morgan, Rockefeller and Vanderbilt. The celebrated New York hostess Mrs E T Stotesbury had several; of her Pennsylvania mansion, Whitemarsh Hall, it was said that when Henry Ford entered it for the first time, he murmured to his wife, 'It's

1931 Phantom II Newmarket convertible sedan, chassis number 220 AJS, coachwork by Brewster, owned by Dr John A Bowers.

instructive to see how the rich live. The much-married millionaire Tommy Manville had no fewer than two Silver Ghosts, five Phantom Is (one of which he gave to his mother), two Phantom IIs and one Phantom III, as well as the last Inskip-bodied Silver Wraith. Among world leaders, ex-President Woodrow Wilson had a 1923 Silver Ghost Oxford seven-passenger touring car, General G M Morales, the President of Cuba, had a 1926 Oxford touring car, and the Polish Marshal Pilsudski had one of the six 1hd Phantom IIs sold in Europe, a Barker-bodied all-weather touring car with two horns, 'very loud', and 'loudest possible', and a 28 gallon gas tank. Hollywood stars and producers were well represented in Springfield's order books, including Jackie Coogan, Anita Loos, Mae Murray, Pola Negri, Gloria Swanson, Tom Mix, Mack Sennett, Norma Talmadge, Al Jolson, Zeppo Marx, Clara Bow and Daryl Zanuck.

The end of the American Rolls-Royce was not of course the end for Rolls-Royce in America, and although in recent years activities have been confined to sales, some measure of individuality was kept going for a while by John S Inskip who took over the sixth floor of the Brewster building for service and bodymaking. Between 1936 and 1945 he built 20 bodies on the Phantom III chassis as well as rebuilding or modifying several British-bodied cars. Among his designs were a revival of the Henley roadster and several sedans, coupés and town cars. At the outbreak of war he moved from the Brewster building to 327 E 64th Street, and in 1945 across the street to 304. These premises became a mecca for Rolls-Royce enthusiasts in the postwar era, for the cars were now attracting a new class of owner, mostly young and not very rich, who loved the cars as pieces of fine machinery. The automobile historian Keith Marvin, who was one of this group, reports that in 1945 Rolls-Royces and other grand cars emerged from their wartime hibernation, but within a few months they were disposed of by their owners and came onto the market for a few hundred dollars each. It was at these East 64th Street premises that Inskip built his last bodies, two four-seat sports roadsters on the Silver Wraith chassis. One of these was the Tommy Manville car already referred to, and Keith recalls stumbling into the bodybuilding shop (on the fourth floor, above a baby food wholesaler) to see this car under construction.

J S Inskip Inc continued to represent Rolls-Royce in America until 1967, but ten years earlier Rolls-Royce Inc had been formed, originally to improve service for customers of aircraft engines, and it was this company which was mainly responsible for sales nationwide. They appointed new distributors in Texas and California, and also launched a new advertising campaign with Ogilvy, Benson & Mather which included the famous 'At 60 miles an hour, the loudest noise in this new Rolls-Royce comes from the electric clock.' This is said to have caused Rolls-Royce engineers to say 'Now we must do something about that damned clock!'

In 1969 new premises for the whole American Rolls-Royce operation were opened at Paramus, New Jersey, and these served for ten years, being replaced in September 1979 by a much larger facility of 90,000 square feet (about three times the size of that at Paramus) at Lyndhurst, New Jersey, only eight miles from Manhattan. Despite the fuel crisis and economic recession, Rolls-Royce sales in North America have grown throughout the 1970s, and are currently running at close to the 1000 per year figure. This is nearly three times the best figure obtained by Springfield in the booming twenties, so the story of Rolls-Royce in America is one of continuing success. They may never have beaten Derby, but they contribute a lot to the prosperity of Crewe.

Wraith, Dawn and Cloud

Above: 1956 Silver Cloud I saloon, chassis number SCG 107, owned by
R C Phillips. A good example of the original Silver Cloud, a car that
looked so handsome that customers were reluctant to pay a lot more for
a special body on a Silver Wraith chassis. Top left: 1946 Silver Wraith
convertible, chassis number WYA 26, coachwork by Inskip, owned by
Judge John C North. This was one of the last two bodies built by the New
York firm of Inskip. This was built for Tommy Manville, and the other, very
similar, for Lawrence Donaldson. Both cars still survive.

The story of the Rolls-Royce-engined Hurricanes and Spitfires in the Battle of Britain is too well-known to be repeated, nor is there space for a detailed study of the aircraft engine department. However, as it became increasingly important from the 1930s onward, and dominated the company's activities in the postwar period, it is worth giving a brief summary of its history.

In his earlier days Henry Royce had not the least interest in flying, while the death of Charles Rolls in an airplane must have turned his indifference to actual hostility. However with the outbreak of the First World War the large factory at Derby had to be kept active, and the manufacture of armored car chassis was not sufficient. Claude Johnson suggested making aircraft engines, and the government chose for Rolls-Royce a V-8 unit of Renault design. It seems that this engine sparked Royce's imagination and indignation in the same way that his Decauville car had done 13 years previously, for he at once got to work and, aided mainly by A G Elliott who was largely responsible for the Phantom III and became chief engineer in 1949, he produced the first Rolls-Royce aircraft engine in less than 12 months. This was the Eagle, a V-12 unit of 20.32-liter capacity, developing 225bhp in its original form, rising to 360bhp by February 1918. Two of these engines were used in the Vickers Vimy in which Alcock and Brown flew the Atlantic in 1919.

Other engines such as the Hawk, Falcon and Goshawk followed, but the next important contribution to history came with the Schneider Cup seaplanes of the 1929 to 1931 period. This cup had been competed for biennially and had been won by a Supermarine seaplane powered by a Napier engine in 1927. Two years later Supermarine asked Rolls-Royce to provide a power unit, and Royce, Hives and Elliott came up with the R, a V-12 unit which gave 1545bhp and enabled the Supermarine S.6 seaplane to win the Trophy for Britain for the second time running. Only one more victory was needed for Britain to become the outright winners, but unfortunately by 1931 the country was in the grip of the depression and the government refused to make any grant at all towards the cost of a new engine.

Rolls-Royce could not fund this themselves and it seemed as if there would be no British entry in the 1931 Schneider Trophy Race. Then the redoubtable Lucy, Lady Houston, came to the rescue. An earnest if sometimes misguided patriot, she was determined that Britain should have the best Air Force in the world, even if the politicians were not. Seeing that the type of airplane used for the Schneider Trophy could be the basis of a fighter, she wrote out a check for £100,000 (worth something like £2 million today) for an RAF team for the Schneider Trophy. Supermarine and Rolls-Royce had only six months to produce their entry, but R J Mitchell produced the Supermarine S.6 and Royce with his team an improved R engine developing 2300bhp. The opposition

Right: 1939 Wraith, chassis number WMB 62, with Thrupp & Maberly limousine body for the late Duke of Gloucester. Note that part of the wing opens with the rear door, and that the Flying Lady has been replaced by a gun turret. Substitutes for the Sprit of Ecstasy were very rare, but not unknown. Lord Louis Mountbatten had a sailor giving a semaphore signal on his 1924 Silver Ghost, and the Queen's Phantom IV has a St George and the Dragon mascot. Below: An early post-war body by Park Ward on a 1947 Silver Wraith chassis.

Main picture: 1939 Wraith saloon, chassis number WLB 35, coachwork by Park Ward, owned by H A Edwards. Although Rowbotham described the Wraith as 'a slightly pregnant 25/30', it incorporated a number of important improvements, including a brand new welded chassis frame and independent front suspension by coil springs and unequal length semi-trailing wishbones.

Far left: Bearing a superficial resemblance to the Mark VI, this is in fact the prototype Bentley 'Scalded Cat' of 1940, with straight-8 B80 engine, which the Duke of Edinburgh borrowed in 1949, and which is said to have led him to order the first of the Phantom IVs. Like most Rolls-Royce prototypes, it was broken up after the company had no more use for it. Left: The first complete car offered by Rolls-Royce was the Mark VI Bentley with standard steel body built to Rolls' instructions by the Pressed Steel Company who still make today's Silver Spirits. This is a 1948 example.

withdrew, which was rather an anticlimax, but the Trophy went to Britain nevertheless, and two hours later Flight-Lieutenant Stainforth set the World Air Speed Record at 378.05mph, raising this later to 407.5mph. This financial encouragement led to the development both of the Supermarine Spitfire fighter and its power unit, the Rolls-Royce Merlin engine, earning for Lady Houston the title 'Fairy Godmother of the RAF.' Henry Royce was made a baronet for his contribution to the 1929 Schneider Trophy victory. After the war they were early into jet engines, with such units as the Nene, Derwent, Avon and Spey. Their factory at Barnoldswick, Yorkshire built the RB (Rolls, Barnoldswick) series, of which the RB211 brought about the downfall of the company in 1971 due to its extremely high development costs.

As part of their expanded program of aircraft engine production, Rolls-Royce built a new factory at Crewe, Cheshire, in 1938, and it was from here that the postwar line of Rolls-Royce and Bentley cars emerged, as Derby was totally given over to aircraft engines. Announced in April 1946, the new models were known as the Silver Wraith and the Mark VI respectively, and shared the same 4257cc six-cylinder engine and four-speed gearbox with synchromesh on three upper speeds. The valve layout was new, being an F-head in which the inlet valves were overhead and the exhaust valves at the side, which was a revival of Henry Royce's layout of 1904.

This engine was part of a range of four, six, and eight-cylinder units with many common components, known as the B engines. The eight had been used in the planned Phantom III replacement, 'Big Bertha' and also in a Bentley code-named 'The Scalded Cat' which was driven by various Rolls-Royce staff members throughout the war, and borrowed by the Duke of Edinburgh in 1949. This engine was used for the limited number of Phantom IV cars made between 1950 and 1956 and also in various commercial vehicles including Dennis fire-engines. Commercial vehicle engines are now an important part of Rolls-Royce business, and are used in such well known trucks as ERF, Foden and Seddon-Atkinson.

The most important difference between the engines as fitted to Rolls and Bentley was that the former had a single Stromberg carburetor and the latter twin SUs, and also a higher lift camshaft. The Silver Wraith was still made only in chassis form, though a number of 'recommended' bodywork styles from well-known firms were shown in their catalog, but the Mark VI Bentley had a standard steel body, a four-door sedan designed by Rolls-Royce, built by the Pressed Steel Company at Cowley, Oxford, and finished in a new body plant at Crewe. There were two main reasons for this break with tradition; economically, a custom-made body was much more expensive, and at a time when high incomes were savagely taxed, costs had to be kept down, and also since sales were aimed at export markets to a much greater extent than in prewar days, the designs had to be tailored to these markets, some of which were quite unsuitable for the traditional ash frame with aluminum panels. The price of a standard Mark VI sedan was £2997; if this seems high compared with the £1510 asked for a 1939 Mark V, the increase was no greater than the general inflation in car prices brought about by the war, and it is salutary to realize that £2997 would hardly buy you the most basic Mini City in the summer of 1982! The Silver Wraith was considerably more expensive, at £1835 for a chassis, and a complete car costing from £3802 to £4409, depending on the bodywork.

Left: 1948 Bentley Mark VI drop head coupe, chassis number B 382 CF, coachwork by H J Mulliner. When the top is lowered the car has a very neat appearance.

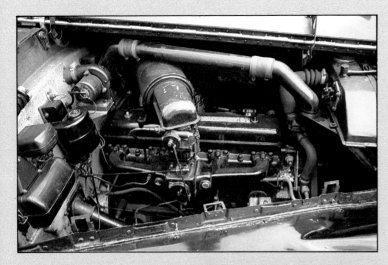

Considering the prevailing austerity of the postwar years, a surprising variety of special bodywork was built on the Silver Wraith chassis, and also the Bentley which was available as a chassis. Up to 1951 the Silver Wraith wheelbase was 127 inches, but in that year a 133 inch wheelbase became available, and within 12 months the shorter one was dropped. Several firms such as Hooper, Park Ward and James Young did their best with the short chassis, but the forward radiator and short length gave most of these early Silver Wraiths a somewhat dumpy look. However, the extra six inches made all the difference, and from 1951 on some very handsome bodywork appeared. H J Mulliner, Hooper and Park Ward, in particular, made superb formal limousines, Freestone & Webb sports sedans, and James Young several examples of that almost obsolete design, the sedanca de ville.

These were mostly made in small series, but the occasional special was ordered as well. Probably the most regular customer for these was Nubar Gulbenkian, son of Calouste Gulbenkian, the Armenian-born oil magnate. Gulbenkian, who seems to have been that rare creature, a genuinely happy millionaire, ordered his first and most striking postwar Rolls-Royce in 1947. This had a Hooper sedanca de ville body with all-enveloping bodywork somewhat reminiscent of a Packard Clipper, wheel spats at front and rear, and a curved radiator grille which largely disguised the car's origin, though the entwined RR and Flying Lady were retained. It is said that the craftsmen at Hooper were distinctly unhappy about building this extraordinary body, but the company was favored by several other orders from Gulbenkian over

Left: 1950 Silver Wraith saloon, chassis number WHD 40, coachwork by Park Ward, owned by Hermione, Lady Colwyn. It has many special features including a hydraulic turntable in the trunk which swings the spare wheel round and drops it to the ground. Above: Engine of the 1950 Silver Wraith; this had the inlet-over-exhaust valve layout which Henry Royce had used on his first car of 1904. Right: Sliding wheel spats, in place of the more usual detachable variety.

Left: 1952 Silver Wraith touring limousine, chassis number WVH 9, coachwork by Hooper. Owned by S Fortune. This was a popular Hooper style, originally known as the Teviot, of which 51 examples were made, differing only in minor details.

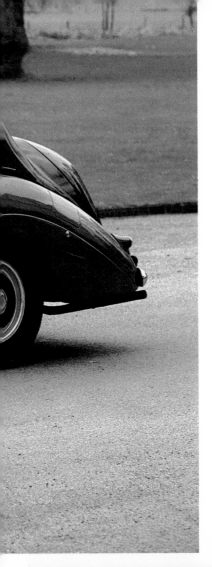

Left and below: 1953 Silver Dawn saloon. This has the big trunk introduced late in 1952 with optional automatic transmission, which was available in the UK market during 1953.

Below left: Harold Radford Countryman conversion to the Silver Dawn, circa 1953. Unlike the later Radford-designed and H J Mulliner-built estate cars on the Silver Cloud, this design preserved the lines of the original saloon. The cost of the conversion was £1105.

the next 12 years, none of them as way-out as the first. These included a four-door convertible on the long wheelbase which was used by the Queen when visiting Nigeria in 1952, a saloon with a clear plastic top built in 1956, and a superb touring limousine on a Phantom V chassis which was ordered just as Hooper was going out of business in 1959, so although designed by their Osmond Rivers it had to be built by Chapron of Paris. Gulbenkian also had a Silver Cloud which was modified from a standard steel sedan to a sedanca de ville by FLM Panelcraft, the small firm who also built his broughams on Austin taxicab chassis. ('I'm told it can turn on a sixpence, whatever that is,' he is supposed to have said of this car.)

The 1950s saw the gradual dwindling of British bodymakers, not only because rising costs made their products uneconomic, but because the older craftsmen were retiring, and there were too few younger men coming along to take their places. Of the famous bodymakers, Freestone & Webb

closed its doors in 1958 and Hooper in 1959, H J Mulliner was taken over by Rolls-Royce and then merged with Park Ward, while James Young survived until 1967. Even building stately limousines was not sufficient to keep the wolf from the door, and Hooper was reduced to making ice cream vans on Austin and Ford chassis at the same time. Nevertheless, about 20 bodymakers, foreign as well as British, worked their craft on the Silver Wraith chassis, a greater number than on any other make of car.

A car which carried some magnificent bodywork was the straight-eight Phantom IV which is said to have had its origin in a visit paid by the Duke of Edinburgh to Crewe in 1949, when he borrowed the Bentley 'Scalded Cat' for an exhilarating drive. He asked Rolls-Royce if it could build a limousine, similarly powered, for himself and Princess Elizabeth, and the result was the first Phantom IV, a massive car on a 145 inch wheelbase and fitted with a limousine body by H J Mulliner. Though mostly used with a chauffeur at the wheel, the Duke drove from time to time and the driver's seat was given sufficient adjustment to accommodate someone of his height. The car was delivered in July 1950, and it was this one vehicle as much as anything which led to the change in Royal favor from Daimler to Rolls-Royce for the official cars. The Duke of Edinburgh's uncle, Earl Mountbatten, had been a Rolls enthusiast since the 1920s, and in this as in other matters he undoubtedly had a great influence on his nephew, and there was also the fact that the Daimler Straight-eight was on the way out and not due to be replaced by anything of comparable size, certainly by 1952 when Princess Elizabeth succeeded to the throne. In the Phantom IV and its successors, the Phantoms V and VI, the Royal Family had a car admirably suited to ceremonial occasions. In fact, the original Mulliner limousine is still to be seen in the Royal Mews today.

A further 15 Phantom IVs were built, all supplied to heads of state either by purchase or as gifts from the British Government. Recipients included General Franco who had two, a limousine and a four-door cabriolet, the Aga Khan, the Sheikh of Kuwait, the King of Iraq, the Prince Regent of Iraq and the Shah of Iran who had two, an H J Mulliner two-door drop-head coupé and a Hooper seven-passenger limousine. The latter was delivered in October 1956 and was the last Phantom IV to be made. At the time of the Shah's flight into exile it was at the Rolls-Royce service depot at Hythe Road, Willesden where it had been sent for extensive renovation, but failing instructions from either the Shah or the Ayatollah's regime, no work was being done on it. The author saw it there in 1979, and it is still there today. Among the British Royal Family, the Queen had another Phantom IV, a Hooper landaulette, while Princess Margaret and the Duke of Gloucester had an H J Mulliner limousine and a Hooper limousine respectively. All bodywork on the Phantom IV chassis was done by these two bodymakers.

As we have said, the Mark VI Bentley could also be provided with special bodywork, and some attractive bodywork was built by most of the leading British firms. As one would expect, the bodies tended to be, if not more sporting, certainly of the owner-driver type, although from the mid-1950s certain standard Hooper and Freestone & Webb styles were common to both chassis, which were virtually identical after the introduction of the Silver Cloud and Bentley S Series in 1955.

One Bentley that really stood out from the crowd was the Continental, particularly in its original R Series form endowed with H J Mulliner fastback coupe bodywork. In the opinion of many car fanciers, this was one of the most beautiful auto-

Left: 1956 Silver Wraith touring limousine, coachwork by H J Mulliner. This design was first built for the 1953 London Motor Show, and carried the curious description of 'All Metal Sports Limousine'. About 12 were made between then and 1956. Right: One of the most unusual designs to be built on the Silver Cloud was this Freestone & Webb two seater drop-head coupe, on chassis number SED 179. It was shown on the coachbuilder's stand at the 1957 London Motor Show, and is now in the United States.

Below: 1957 Silver Wraith limousine, chassis number FLW 34, coachwork by Hooper, owned by J L Harvey. A classic seven-passenger formal limousine, this design was first built by Hooper in 1952. A total of 43 examples was made between then and July 1959.

mobiles ever made. It was the work of Ivan Evernden who had come to prominence with the 'sports' Phantom Is of 1925–8, and stylist J P Blatchley. The engine was the 4566cc six-cylinder unit which had replaced the original 4257cc engine in 1951, and this was mildly tuned though not so much as to interfere with the traditional refinement of Crewe products. However there is no doubt that an R-type Continental under hard acceleration does give a little more indication of its presence than a standard Bentley or a Silver Wraith, but it is no less attractive for that. Evernden had been given instructions that the car should have a top speed of at least 120mph, more than 20 percent above the standard Mark VI, and his main weapons in obtaining this were lightness of construction and aerodynamic form. Blatchley came up with a beautiful sloping back design which some detractors have tried to compare with a 1949 Chevrolet Fleetline, but which is in fact infinitely more lithe and delicate.

When first road tested by *The Autocar* in September 1952 the prototype Continental recorded a top speed of 116.9mph, and fuel consumption of 19.4mpg. This prototype was registered OLG 490 and was inevitably christened 'Olga'. She was used for eight years by various members of the Rolls-Royce staff, and among outsiders who drove her was the well-known Bentley enthusiast and President of the Bentley Drivers Club, Stanley Sedgwick. He intimated that when the company had finished with Olga he would be very happy to acquire her, but was told that it was company policy to break up prototypes when they no longer had any use for them. However, they made an exception in this case, and in December 1960 Stanley took delivery of a distinctly down-at-heel Olga who had covered nearly 250,000 far from gentle miles. With the aid of the Rolls-Royce service depot, and H J Mulliner and Wood & Pickett who did the retrimming, she was restored to her former glory, and has since covered well over 100,000 additional miles including many continental tours.

A total of 208 R-type Continentals were made, of which all but 16 had H J Mulliner bodywork similar to Olga's, apart from a one-piece windshield in place of her divided one. Of the others, some were bodied by Abbott of Farnham (coupé) or Park Ward (convertible), while a few went to Continental bodymakers such as Graber of Switzerland or Pininfarina of Italy. There were only two major changes during the model's

lifetime, both of which applied to other Bentley and Rolls-Royce cars as well. These were a further increase in engine size, to 4887cc, in 1954, and the option of automatic transmission in 1953. Left-hand-drive cars with manual shift had a steering column gearshift unless a central floor shift was particularly requested. All right-hand-drive cars had the right hand gearshift.

Apart from the three Le Mans appearances of the prewar Embiricos Bentley, Rolls' sporting activities have been limited to rallies. Several Bentleys and Silver Wraiths took part in the Monte Carlo Rally in the 1950s, aiming their sights at the Concours de Confort rather than any outright awards. The best-known exponent of these activities was W M (Mike) Couper, a Hertfordshire garage owner who entered a standard Mark VI Bentley saloon in 1949, and 1951 to 1953, winning the Grand Prix d'Honneur de Confort in 1949, 1951 and 1952, while he entered a Park Ward-bodied Silver Wraith saloon in 1950, also winning the Grand Prix.

In 1949 the standard steel body of the Bentley was mated to a Rolls-Royce radiator to produce a car aimed particularly at the American market, and christened the Silver Dawn. The thinking behind it was to meet the demand for the prestige of Rolls-Royce ownership combined with a more compact body than the Silver Wraith's, and one which was essentially for the man who drove himself. Chauffeurs were even rarer in postwar America than they were in Britain.

For the 1953 season the Dawn and Mark VI were given a larger trunk which improved their appearance, while the general improvements of larger engine and option of automatic transmission were made on the Dawn as on the Silver Wraith. By October 1953 the Dawn was available on the UK market, and it remained in production until the Spring of 1955 when it was replaced by the Silver Cloud. Like the Bentley it was available as a chassis only, and a number of custom bodies were built on it for those who wanted an individual body on a wheelbase seven inches shorter than that of the original Silver Wraith, and 13 inches less than the long wheelbase Wraith.

The introduction of automatic transmission caused a certain amount of head shaking among the old school, both owner-drivers and chauffeurs, and some people were particularly distressed that the system adopted by Rolls-Royce was a copy of a General Motors design, such as could be found on

any Pontiac or Oldsmobile. However Rolls-Royce engineers have never been averse to adopting a good design from elsewhere, but they have always insisted on improving the product, and above all on making it to their standards, which is why they build the gearbox at Crewe rather than importing it complete from Detroit. A four-speed Hydramatic system, it was introduced in 1952 on the export models of the Bentley, and two years later manual shifts could be had only on the Continentals.

Since at least 1950 Rolls-Royce had been working on a replacement for the Silver Dawn and Mark VI Bentley, and this appeared in April 1955 under the name Silver Cloud and S Series Bentley (the larger-engined big trunk models had been known as the R Series). The new models had the larger 4887cc engine first seen on the 1954 Bentley Continental, now endowed with an entirely new light-alloy cylinder head.

The bodies, designed by Rolls-Royce and built by Pressed Steel, were completely new, though the fender line owed something to certain H J Mulliner designs dating back to 1951. They were roomier, both in passenger compartment and trunk, than their predecessors, and were three inches longer in wheelbase, at 123 inches. A longer model, with 127 inch wheelbase, was introduced in 1957 for special body-work. Rolls-Royce resisted the temptation to go for integral construction of chassis and body because they wanted to be able to offer a chassis for custom built bodies, and also because the tooling costs would be too great for a design which they did not envisage lasting for more than ten years or 20,000 units. They were pretty accurate in their production span forecast, for the Silver Cloud was made until September 1965, but somewhat over-optimistic on production figures, for the total number of Cloud and Bentley steel bodied sedans

Above: 1955 Bentley R-type Continental coupe, chassis number BC 4E, coachwork by H J Mulliner, owned by John Hampton. This was the last R-type Continental to be delivered. Top left: 1958 Silver Wraith limousine, chassis number HLW 38, coachwork by Hooper, owned by Paget LW Bellin. Top right: Hooper touring limousine on a late Silver Wraith chassis, number GLW 14, delivered in April 1958.

made was 12,922. When various custom built bodies, including Bentley Continentals, are added, the figure still does not exceed 14,929.

The Silver Cloud and S Series Bentley used the same engine, and indeed there was now no difference between the cars apart from the radiators, but Rolls-Royce customers had to pay £130 more for their cars. Some of this, at least, was accounted for by the extra labor involved in making the Rolls radiator and Flying Lady. Quite a number of custom built bodies were put on the Silver Cloud chassis, particularly after the introduction of the longer wheelbase in 1957. Most of the surviving British firms tried their hand, Freestone & Webb and Hooper, in particular, evolving striking designs with flowing lines, fender-mounted headlights and enclosed rear wheels. An unusual design, based on the standard steel sedan, was the Harold Radford estate car, surely the ultimate

in country gentlemen's conveyances. This company had also made a few Countryman sedans derived from the Silver Dawn, but these preserved the sedan's lines.

The Bentley Continental was continued in the S Series, although the differences between it and the Rolls-Royce were not so marked as before, apart from the bodywork. From 1956 to 1957 the Continental had a higher compression ratio, but otherwise the engines were virtually identical. Bodywork on the Continental was shared among H J Mulliner, Park Ward and James Young. Mulliner's S 1 coupé was in the same style as their R-type, but something of the inimitable flair of the former was lost, and the car had a rather heavier appearance. They also made a four-door sports sedan named the Flying Spur, and this style was also made by James Young with subtle differences.

Park Ward made coupes and convertibles, and in 1959

they introduced the first bodies on Rolls-Royce or Bentley to have absolutely straight-through lines from headlight to tail. Four headlights were featured on the 1963 models, in line with their adoption on the regular Silver Cloud, but in the case of the Park Ward bodies they were mounted outboard and in slightly slanting style. Most of the Continental body styles were also available with the Rolls-Royce radiator, with the exception of the Mulliner coupe, so that it is possible to find Flying Spur Silver Clouds, though they are very rare. The last Continental was delivered to the bodymaker on 29 November 1965, and was not sold to the customer until the end of January 1966, four months after the model had been officially replaced by the Bentley T Series.

By the end of the 1950s it was obvious that the old six-cylinder engine with its 'magic' dimension of 4.150 inches between the centers of the cylinder bores was coming to the end of its development. With the final enlargement of this unit to 4887cc, the bores were so close together that it was no longer possible to run the cooling water between them. Consideration was given to using the B80 straight-eight engine that powered the Phantom IV, but this was too long and too heavy, so the obvious solution was to adopt the V-8 layout which was universal on the larger American cars. A V-8 is compact and light, and can be developed in size with relative ease. The new engine, which appeared in the Silver Cloud II and Bentley S2 in September 1959, was considerably larger than any Rolls engine since the Phantom III, with a capacity of 6230cc. However it was 10lbs lighter than its predecessor, thanks to light alloy construction of the cylinder block, and with an identical body and chassis the new car was some 15mph faster and had markedly better acceleration. The engine remained virtually unchanged until 1970 when it was enlarged to 6750cc.

Automatic transmission was standard on the Silver Cloud II, and in fact the last cars to be delivered with a stick shift were S1 Continentals in early 1957. Power steering, introduced as an option on export cars in April 1956, was now standard. The final development of the Silver Cloud came in October 1962 with the Cloud III and its accompanying Bentley S3. These had about 8 percent more power thanks to a higher compression ratio, and were externally distinguishable by four headlights and a lower hood line.

Even after the introduction of the Silver Cloud, the Silver Wraith had remained in small-scale production for those who wanted a long chassis on which to mount formal bodywork. The demand for such cars was fast dwindling, and it might have been expected that the Wraith would have been allowed to fade quietly away, with no replacement. However, at the same time as the launch of the V-8 engine, Rolls-Royce announced a new chassis expressly intended for limousine bodies. Christened the Phantom V, its chassis was a lengthened version of the Silver Cloud, with a wheelbase of 144 inches and an overall length of 238 inches. Although the wheelbase was one inch less than that of the Phantom IV, the car was longer, wider and heavier, and was the largest Rolls-Royce ever built. Engine, transmission and steering were identical to those on the Silver Cloud, but their final drive ratio was lower to provide a creeping speed appropriate for ceremonial occasions.

Of course the bodymakers had been told in advance of the new model, and the Earls Court Motor Show in October 1959 saw seven Phantom Vs in the Hooper, H J Mulliner, Park Ward and James Young exhibits, as well as Rolls-Royce. These were the only surviving traditional British bodymakers, and Hooper had already announced it was to close the following year. Hooper made only one body on the Phantom V, a

Right: 1962 Silver Cloud II saloon. This is the intermediate model of Silver Cloud with the V-8 engine introduced in 1959, but the same external appearance as the Cloud I of 1955.

Below: 1965 Silver Cloud III coupe, chassis number CEL 19, coachwork by James Young. This is a unique body, and although built by James Young the rear windows are very reminiscent of Hooper. It was described in the James Young order book as a Touring Limousine.
Below right: 1963 Silver Cloud III saloon. The final model in the Silver Cloud series, this is quickly identified by its quad headlights and a slightly lower radiator. Introduced for the 1963 model year, it was replaced in October 1965 by the Silver Shadow.

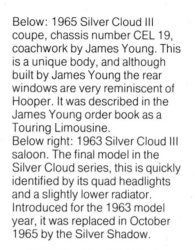

formal seven-passenger limousine, although it designed a more exotic touring limousine for Nubar Gulbenkian which was built by Chapron in Paris under the strict supervision of Osmond Rivers, Hooper's chief designer.

H J Mulliner and Park Ward, both now owned by Rolls-Royce, were amalgamated in 1961, and the only subsequent bodies on the Phantom V were made by them or James Young which survived as part of Jack Barclay Limited until 1967. Most bodies were limousines but Young built four sedanca de villes in the early 1960s, which must have been the last of this design made anywhere in the world. In 1960 Park Ward built a very special limousine for Queen Elizabeth II. Named

'Canberra,' this was a limousine with a plastic roof and rear section to give a better view of the occupants, with a roof level five inches higher than on the standard limousine. For privacy when not on parade, the car was equipped with aluminum panels to cover the plastic; normally kept in the trunk, these took less than a minute to put in place. This car, together with a second built in 1961, are still in regular use by the Royal Family.

The drastic inflation in Rolls-Royce prices will be covered in the next chapter, but it is worth pointing out that when introduced, the Park Ward Phantom V limousine cost £8905 with tax, and the James Young limousine £9394. These were considered astronomical at the time, yet today one pays a similar sum for a middle-of-the-range Ford Granada.

A total of 832 Phantom Vs were made up to the autumn of 1968 when they were replaced by the generally similar Phantom VI. This was equipped with separate air-conditioning in front and rear compartments, and has been made in small numbers up to the present day. Around 385 have been made to date, and recent production has been extremely limited. In 1981 14 cars were delivered, and in the first half of 1982, six. Even the Phantom VI now has a standard body, a seven-passenger limousine by H J Mulliner/Park Ward, and although a great variety of extras is offered there is no deviation from the standard body. The landaulette is still available, but none has been ordered for more than 12 months. The last 'special' was a limousine with a 'Canberra' top which was the gift of the British Motor Industry to the Queen on the occasion of her Silver Jubilee in 1977. Phantom VI bodies are constructed at the Hythe Road plant in North West London which Mulliner/Park Ward shares with the service department and the School of Instruction. The chassis, engine and gearbox come from Crewe, but suspensions and steering gears are mounted at Hythe Road. All the aluminum panels are hammered by hand, and the number of man hours involved in completing a Phantom VI body is well over 800. Since 1974 no price has been quoted for the Phantom VI as this varies so much with the extra features required by customers. At the time of writing, in the summer of 1982, it could not be less than £125,000, and could well be as high as £140,000. A landaulette would cost at least £160,000.

Above: 1975 Camargue coupe, chassis number JRH 30015, owned by Rolls-Royce Motors Limited. This is the most expensive Rolls-Royce made, apart from the built-to-order Phantom VI, and currently retails at £83,122. Not more than 100 are made each year. Top: interior appointments of the Camargue are to the highest standards, with burr walnut veneer panelling for fascia and doors, leather trim and deep pile Wilton carpets. Although it has only two doors, the Camargue is a full five-passenger car.

Silver Shadow to Silver Spirit

Scarcely had the Silver Cloud entered production in the Spring of 1955 than consideration was being given to its successor. It was decided that this must be a car with more compact exterior dimensions and yet with greater interior space. Most of the Silver Cloud's contemporaries were already lower, and for a car that was not to be introduced until the 1960s a low roof line was an essential requirement. It could be argued that the Cloud's height gave it a dignity and distinction appropriate to Rolls-Royce, but the company was well aware of changing tastes, and that a majority of customers no longer wanted a dignified dinosaur but a car which, while sacrificing nothing in quality, was less obtrusive in the parking lot, and, both figuratively and literally, maintained a lower profile. The demands of a compact exterior and a roomy interior virtually dictated integral construction of chassis and body, and anyway this was becoming the accepted way in which to build cars, and one which suited Pressed Steel which was to be retained as the company's suppliers. So the epoch-making step toward integral construction, which had been firmly rejected only five years earlier, was taken, and was the most important feature of the new car.

Hardly less important, though, was the independent suspension of the rear wheels as well as the front, and the self-leveling system which was developed. IRS gave improved riding comfort and greater space in the rear compartment, but also allowed greater deflection of the springs than on previous models. To maintain the car on an even keel what-ever the load, a hydraulically-operated height control system driven by the engine was designed, so that when passengers entered the car, or the trunk was loaded with luggage, the car swiftly regained its former height, at the rate of about half an inch per second. The work was performed by four hydraulic pistons, those at the rear having a total travel of three inches, though this was seldom utilized unless five heavy passengers and a full complement of luggage were being carried. After 1969 the front pistons were dispensed with. Another major step forward was the adoption of disk brakes all around, with three separate hydraulic circuits, as well as a mechanical handbrake.

The prototype was on the road by the summer of 1957, and several others followed, but it was to be eight years before the car was deemed ready for the marketplace. By then the V-8 engine had been standardized on the Clouds, and this power unit was used in the new cars with little change apart from making the sparkplugs more accessible. Announced in October 1965, the new models were christened the Rolls-Royce Silver Shadow and the Bentley T Series. The latter were identical with the Rolls-Royce apart from the radiator, but they cost £60 less at £6496 including tax. The new cars were five inches lower, seven inches shorter and three and a half inches narrower than the Silver Cloud, and the radiators were shallower, approaching the proportions of the pre-1910 Silver Ghost.

Interestingly, the new cars were launched at the Paris

Left: Even the Maharajahs of old did not buy as many as eight Rolls-Royces at a time, but this was the order of Horace Kadoorie of the Peninsula Group of Hotels in Hong Kong. The cars are used for carrying guests to and from the airport, and for other duties; Mr Kadoorie is seen (left) taking delivery at Crewe in June 1976. No, he did not get a discount for a bulk order.

Below: The adoption of integral construction on the Silver Shadow and T Series Bentley virtually put an end to special coachwork, but Pininfarina managed to produce this coupe on the T Series for the 1968 Paris and London Shows. Main picture: 1978 Corniche convertible, chassis number DRH 30003, coachwork by H J Mulliner/Park Ward. This model gave Rolls-Royce a younger image than any of their previous models, and has proved very popular with stars of the film, fashion and pop music world.

Salon, a parallel with the first 10hp Rolls-Royce of 1904. When tested by *Autocar* in 1967 the Shadow was found to be fractionally slower in top speed and acceleration than the Cloud III, as the mechanical complexities made it a little heavier despite the smaller overall size. However, rapid acceleration has never been the first consideration to a Rolls-Royce customer, and it is unlikely that they lost any sales because of this shortcoming, which was soon made good anyway when the larger engine was introduced. More serious was the criticism of the power-assisted recirculating ball steering system which many drivers found to be lacking in feel. *Autocar* reported that the steering wheel had to be moved up to a sixth of a turn before the car reacted at all, and that strong side winds and uneven camber made the car lurch from side to side before the driver could check it. This steering was said to have been developed with American drivers in mind, but it is significant that it was replaced by a rack-and-pinion layout on the Silver Shadow 2 introduced in 1977.

At first the Silver Shadow was made only as a four-door sedan, but a few variations appeared over the next four years. James Young converted 50 cars to two-door sedans, some of them with Bentley radiators, using the same body lines as the standard four-door model. More individual in appearance was the two-door sedan from H J Mulliner/Park Ward which was introduced in March 1966 and joined by a convertible version in September 1967. These were considerably more expensive, at £9849 and £10,511 respectively, but this was inevitable as they were made in smaller numbers, and the convertible had to have a greatly strengthened center section to compensate for the loss of rigidity caused by the absence of a steel roof. The complex machinery for operating the powered opening and closing of the roof also added to the cost and weight, but these convertibles were (and are) important for Rolls-Royce as they gave the company a new, younger image which fitted well with the whole mystique of 'Swinging London' which was at its height in the late 1960s. Rolls-Royces had been popular with successful actors and movie stars for a long time, but they were a trifle too staid and square for the new generation of pop star. The convertible, which became the Corniche in 1971, changed all that, and soon became highly desirable transport for countless stars as well as younger businessmen for whom the car was a unique combination of status symbol and blue-chip investment.

A month before the announcement of the Corniche came the news, almost as incredible as the collapse of the Bank of England, that Rolls-Royce Limited had called in a receiver and were, in effect, bankrupt. There is no room here to go into the details of how this came about, but it was in no way the responsibility of the Car Division, but rather because the Aero Engine Division could not meet a huge order from Lockheed for the RB 211 engine at the originally quoted price. The contract did not allow them to raise the price, and the discrepancy between their costs and their returns were so great that bankruptcy was the only answer. The Aero Engine Division, which had sustained the cars for many years, now threatened to drag them down into oblivion. Rumors abounded of purchasers from Britain and abroad. Would Rolls-Royce become part of British Leyland? Of Mercedes-Benz? Or even of a Japanese company?

In any event, the receiver took the bold step of separating the Car Division from the Aero Engine Division, which was then nationalized. He suggested the floatation of a new public company to be known as Rolls-Royce Motors Limited, and this came into being in May 1973, headed by David Plastow,

Two models of the Corniche, a convertible, chassis number DRH 30003, owned by Rolls-Royce Motors Limited (above right), and a coupe, chassis number CRH 25261, owned by Harvey Herbert (below). This was first registered on January 1st 1977, and has the latest split-level air conditioning and twin exhaust system.

the young and very successful sales director of the former Car Division. Meanwhile the launch of new models went on. The Corniches were brought out at a lavish presentation at Nice, an appropriate location for a model named after the roads which link Nice and Monte Carlo. In appearance they were little changed from the previous two-door sedan and convertible, but the engines were tuned to give about 10 percent more power, which gave the cars a significant improvement in performance over the Silver Shadow. Top speed was now in excess of 120mph compared with 116mph for the Shadow, and 0–60 acceleration improved from 10.9 seconds to 9.6.

The Corniche was built in much smaller numbers than the Shadow, and customers soon had to wait as much as four years for delivery, which naturally led to a flourishing black market in low-mileage secondhand models. In 1974 a new Corniche convertible listed at £16,278, yet buyers were prepared to pay several thousands above this figure for immediate delivery, and more than one car sold for as much as £28,000 at auction. This naturally encouraged speculators to buy a new Corniche and sell it for a tidy profit within a few weeks, but Rolls-Royce dealers kept a careful watch on this sort of thing, and as a spokesman at Jack Barclay Ltd said,

anyone found making a quick profit would never be sold another car. This situation applied to a lesser extent to all Rolls-Royce models in the mid-1970s, which meant that if an owner changed his car every twelve months, his motoring was virtually cost-free once he had paid the initial price. Admittedly new car prices rose steadily, but as a low-mileage secondhand model had a premium of at least £2000 over its cost, the inflation was just about canceled out. This applied to no other make of car, and led to a number of business firms choosing Rolls-Royce for their company cars as they were the only items on the books to show no depreciation.

The Silver Shadow sedan was steadily improved over the years, and it is said that more than 2000 modifications were made between 1965 and 1977. Most important of these were the adoption of a torque converter and three-speed automatic transmission in place of the fluid coupling and four speeds (July 1968), standardization of air-conditioning (November 1969), a larger engine of 6750cc (July 1970) and the replacement of crossply tires by radials (August 1972). These were again changed for wider profile tires in April 1974, when a pronounced wheel flare on the body sides was made to accommodate the new tires. In February

1977 came the Silver Shadow II which apart from the rack-and-pinion steering already mentioned had a wheelbase half an inch longer, a deeper radiator shell with air dam beneath it and split-level air-conditioning which had already been introduced on the Camargue. A month later it was joined by a longer-wheelbase version christened the Silver Wraith II which could be had with a division between driver and passengers. This cost £4087 more than the Shadow II, but it provided a suitably dignified car for chauffeur drive at a great deal less than the Phantom VI.

In March 1975 Rolls-Royce took the bold step of introducing a new model which cost nearly £10,000 more than the Corniche. This was the Camargue, a two-door saloon styled by Sergio Pininfarina and which was commissioned by the company in 1969. It was intended to be less sporting than the Corniche, but simply to be the ultimate in owner-driver cars. In fact, it has taken over the mantle of the Corniche sedan which was quietly dropped during 1981. Unlike the Corniche, the Camargue is not built by Mulliner/Park Ward (though it was originally), but has its own 'production line' at Crewe where not more than 100 are made each year. The floor pan is similar to that of other Rolls-Royces and is made by Pressed Steel, but the upper part of the structure is made by Motor Panels of Coventry who weld it to the floor before sending the completed unit to Crewe for finishing. The upholstery is, of course, all leather, including the door panels and seat backs, and each Camargue uses more than £1000 worth of the finest Connolly hides.

Unlike the Corniche, the Camargue was intended purely as a Rolls-Royce, with no Bentley equivalent, though David Plastow said at the time of its introduction 'If anyone asked us for a Bentley, we would certainly quote him a price.' So far, no one has. The price in March 1975 was £29,250, compared with £19,867 for a Corniche convertible, £19,013 for a Corniche sedan and only £14,829 for a Silver Shadow. Within a year the Camargue had risen to £34,006 and another twelve months took it up to £40,353. At the time of writing (July 1982) the price is £83,122, or an increase of 284 percent in seven years. Over the same period, a Corniche has risen from £19,867 to £73,168, a 368 percent increase, and the current Silver Spirit, the Shadow's replacement, costs £55,500, or 374 percent above 1975's price. These increases are far above that of the general cost of living, though they are not way out of line from other cars (a basic Mini has risen by 292 percent and a Jaguar XJ12 by 345 percent).

The Silver Shadow was the most successful Rolls-Royce

Right and below: 1979 Silver
Shadow II, chassis number SRH
30427, owned by Leslie Benton.
Introduced in February 1977, the
Shadow II differed from its
predecessor in having a
wheelbase half an inch longer, and
deeper radiator shell and the split
level air-conditioning that had
already been introduced on the
Camargue.

ever made, in terms of sales, and when it was replaced in 1980 it had sold more than 32,000 units. Fewer than 10 percent of these had been Bentleys, a complete reversal of the early post-war situation when the Bentley Mark VI had easily outsold the Silver Wraith and Silver Dawn. One of the decisions made when planning the Shadow's successor was that the Bentley should be given greater individuality in the new range, and this eventually came about. Announced in the fall of 1980, the new cars were named the Silver Spirit and Bentley Mulsanne, the latter being named after the Mulsanne Straight at Le Mans, where Bentleys won the 24 Hour Race five times in the 1920s. Their styling was the work of Austrian-born Fritz Feller, Chief Engineer of Styling and Future Projects, and showed a strong influence of the Camargue, particularly at the front end, though the radiator does not have the 10° forward lean of the Camargue. The body has a heavier look to it than that of the Shadow and gives the impression of more car for the money, though it is in fact only 2.3 inches wider, 2.9 inches longer and 1.3 inches lower. The waistline has been considerably lowered and the window area increased by 30 percent. Following the tradition of providing a more formal version of their standard sedan, Rolls-Royce offers the longer-wheelbase Silver Spur as a replacement for the Silver Wraith II. The engine and transmission are little changed from the Shadows, though fuel injection replaces the twin SU carburetors for the American and Japanese markets.

The long-awaited high-performance Bentley was announced in the Spring of 1982. Named the Mulsanne Turbo,

Above: 1982 Bentley Mulsanne Turbo saloon, owned by Rolls-Royce Motors Limited. The most sporting car to carry the Bentley name since the R-type Continental, the Mulsanne Turbo has approximately 50% more power than the standard version, and 0 to 60mph acceleration in 7.4 seconds. The price in the Spring of 1983 was £61,243, compared with £55,240 for the unblown Mulsanne. Below: 1981 Silver Spirit saloon, owned by Rolls-Royce Motors Limited. The current 'standard' Rolls-Royce, the Silver Spirit has 30% more glass area than the Shadow. It has power adjustment for reach, tilt and height on the front seats, and among the information provided by the digital display panel is outside temperature.

this employs a Garrett AiResearch turbocharger energized by the exhaust gases, which forces air through the single Solex downdraft carburetor. This gives an approximate 50 percent increase in power, from around 200 to 300bhp, and an acceleration from 0 to 60mph in $7\frac{1}{2}$ seconds. Top speed is limited to 135mph by a sensor which restricts turbo boost. Like the R-type Continental, the Turbo is decidedly noisier than the equivalent Rolls-Royce, but this is unlikely to deter potential customers. The company is adamant that the Turbo will never carry a Rolls-Royce radiator, and in fact it has been calculated that if it did it would need an extra 35bhp to achieve the same performance, because of the additional drag of the square shell. The Turbo's radiator is the same shape as that of the ordinary Mulsanne, but is distinguished by being painted in the color of the car, rather than silver. Production is deliberately limited, and it is the only Rolls-Royce model for which there is currently a substantial waiting list; all 1982's allocation of 100 cars had already been sold by July of that year. So far it is not available on the US, Australian or Japanese markets as it does not meet emission control regulations in those countries, but an injected version that does is being planned.

There, for the moment, the Rolls-Royce story rests. The future is not as rosy as it was a few years ago, and gone are the days of three-year waiting lists and premiums of several thousand pounds for immediate delivery. Today one can get almost immediate delivery of any model apart from the Turbo, and the only wait would be for a particular color scheme. However this should be seen in the light of increased production, which went up from 2850 in 1980 to 3175 in 1981, despite a drop of just under 10 percent in the workforce at Crewe. Exports were up by 26 percent, even if home sales were slightly down. Fear that a workforce facing being laid off might resent the purchase of a new Rolls-Royce by their company do not seem to have been born out. In two such cases the employees were asked whether they thought the company should have a new Rolls-Royce or switch to a cheaper car, and both voted overwhelmingly in favor of a new Rolls. This is clearly encouraging, for about 70 percent of British sales are to companies rather than individual buyers.

A few years ago, the well-known journalist John Bolster asked Rolls Royce Chief Engineer John Hollings what the successor to the Silver Shadow would be like, 'but the only detail I could extract was that the next model will have a radiator!' One can be reasonably certain that the Spirit's successor will also have a radiator, a front-mounted engine driving the rear wheels and a body capable of carrying four to five people in as much comfort as any other car on the road.

Anything more is speculation, but as always with Rolls-Royce, the new model will probably come in two stages, a fresh and probably smaller engine perhaps in 1985/6, and a new body shell two or three years after that. What is beyond doubt is that it will maintain the standards of its predecessors, and that the famous, the successful and all lovers of fine workmanship will continue to be proud to drive behind the figure of the Flying Lady.

Appendix

1904 Royce 10hp
2 cylinders 95.25 × 127mm 1809cc
3 forward speeds
wheelbase: 75 inches
number made: 3

1904–1906 Rolls-Royce 10hp
2 cylinders 95.25 × 127mm (100 ×
127 on later cars) 1809cc (1995cc)
3 forward speeds
wheelbase: 75 inches
number made: 16

1905 Rolls-Royce 15hp
3 cylinders 101.6 × 127mm 3089cc
3 forward speeds
wheelbase: 103 inches
number made: 6

1905–1908 Rolls-Royce 20hp
4 cylinders 101.6 × 127mm 4118cc
4 cylinders 101.6 × 127mm 4118cc
3 forward speeds ('heavy' model)
4 forward speeds ('light' model)
wheelbase: 106 or 114 inches
number made: 40

1905–1906 Rolls-Royce 30hp
6 cylinders 101.6 × 127mm 6177cc
4 forward speeds
wheelbase: 116½ or 118 inches
number made: 37

1905–1906 Rolls-Royce V-8
8 cylinders 82.6 × 82.6mm 3535cc
3 forward speeds
wheelbase: 90 or 106 inches
number made: 3, and parts of a fourth

**1907–1925 Rolls-Royce 40/50hp
Silver Ghost**
6 cylinders 114.3 × 114.3mm
7036cc (1907–1909)
114.3 × 120.7mm 7428cc
(1909–1925)
4 forward speeds, direct drive in third
(1907–1909)
3 forward speeds /1909–1913)
4 forward speeds, direct drive in high
(1913–1925)
wheelbase: 135½, 143½, 144 or 150½
inches
number made: 6173

**1921–1926 Rolls-Royce 40/50hp
Silver Ghost (Springfield)**
6 cylinders 114.3 × 120.7mm 7428cc
4 forward speeds
wheelbase: 144 or 150½ inches
number made: 1703

1922–1929 Rolls-Royce 20hp
6 cylinders 76.2 × 114.3mm 3127cc
3 forward speeds (1922–1925)
4 forward speeds (1925–1929)
wheelbase: 129 inches
number made: 2940

**1925–1929 Rolls-Royce 40/50hp
New Phantom (Phantom I)**
6 cylinders 108 × 139.7mm 7668cc
4 forward speeds
wheelbase: 143½ or 150½ inches
number made: 2212

**1926–1931 Rolls-Royce 40/50hp
New Phantom (Phantom I)
(Springfield)**
6 cylinders 108 × 139.7mm 7668cc
4 forward speeds
wheelbase: 143½ or 146½ inches
number made: 1241

1929–1936 Rolls-Royce 20/25hp
6 cylinders 82.6 × 114.3mm 3669cc
4 forward speeds
wheelbase: 129 or 132 inches
number made: 3827

**1929–1935 Rolls-Royce 40/50hp
Phantom II**
6 cylinders 108 × 139.7mm 7668cc
4 forward speeds
wheelbase: 144 or 150 inches
number made: 1767
1933–1936 Bentley 3½ liter
6 cylinders 82.6 × 114.3mm 3669cc
4 forward speeds
wheelbase: 126 inches
number made: 1191
1936–1939 Bentley 4¼ liter
6 cylinders 88.9 × 114.3mm 4257cc
4 forward speeds
wheelbase: 126 inches
number made: 1241
1939–1941 Bentley Mark V
6 cylinders 88.9 × 114.3mm 4257cc
4 forward speeds
wheelbase: 124 inches
number made: less than 20
**1936–1939 Rolls-Royce 40/50hp
Phantom III**
12 cylinders 82.5 × 114.3mm 7340cc
4 forward speeds
wheelbase: 142 inches
number made: 710
1936–1938 Rolls-Royce 25/30hp
6 cylinders 88.9 × 114.3mm 4257cc
4 forward speeds
wheelbase: 132 inches
number made: 1201

1938–1939 Rolls-Royce Wraith
6 cylinders 88.9 × 114.3mm 4257cc
4 forward speeds
wheelbase: 126 inches
number made: 491
**1946–1955 Bentley Mark VI and
R-type**
6 cylinders 88.9 × 114.3mm 4257cc
(1946–1951)
92.1 × 114.3mm 4566cc (1951–1954)
95.25 × 114.3mm 4887cc
(1954–1955 Continental)
4 forward speeds (4 speed automatic
optional from 1952)
wheelbase: 120 inches
number made: 5946 Mark VI, 2320
R-type, 207 R-type Continental
**1946–1959 Rolls-Royce Silver
Wraith**
6 cylinders 88.9 × 114.3mm 4257cc
(1946–1951)
92.1 × 114.3mm 4566cc (1951–1954)
95.25 × 114.3mm 4887cc
(1954–1959)
4 forward speeds (4 speed automatic
optional from 1952)
wheelbase: 127 or 133 inches
number made: 1783
1949–1955 Rolls-Royce Silver Dawn
6 cylinders 88.9 × 114.3mm 4257cc
(1949–1951)
92.1 × 114.3mm 4566cc (1951–1955)
4 forward speeds (4 speed automatic
optional from 1952)
wheelbase: 120 inches
number made: 760

1950–1956 Rolls-Royce Phantom IV
8 cylinders 88.9 × 114.3mm 5675cc
4 forward speeds
wheelbase: 145 inches
number made: 16
**1955–1959 Rolls-Royce Silver
Cloud I and Bentley S1**
6 cylinders 95.25 × 114.3mm 4887cc
4 forward speeds (automatic)
wheelbase: 123 or 127 inches
number made: 2359 Silver Cloud,
3477 S1
**1959–1962 Rolls-Royce Silver
Cloud II and Bentley S2**
8 cylinders 104.4 × 91.44mm 6230cc
4 forward speeds (automatic)
wheelbase: 123 or 127 inches
number made: 2716 Silver Cloud II,
2308 S2
**Rolls-Royce Silver
Cloud III and Bentley S3**
8 cylinders 104.4 × 91.44mm 6230cc
4 forward speeds (automatic)
wheelbase: 123 or 127 inches
number made: 2376 Silver Cloud III,
1614 S3
1959–1968 Rolls-Royce Phantom V
8 cylinders 104.4 × 91.44mm 6230cc
4 forward speeds (automatic)
wheelbase: 144 inches
number made: 832

1968 to date Rolls-Royce Phantom VI
8 cylinders 104.4mm × 99mm 6750cc
(1979 to date)
3 forward speeds (automatic) (from
1979)
**1965–1977 Rolls-Royce Silver
Shadow I and Bentley T1**
8 cylinders 104.4 × 91.44mm 6320cc
(1965–1970)
104.4 × 99mm 6750cc (1970–1977)
4 forward speeds (automatic)
(1965–1968)
3 forward speeds (automatic)
(1968–1977)
wheelbase: 119½ or 123½ inches
number made: 20,604 Silver Shadow I,
1867 Bentley T1
**1971 to date Rolls-Royce and Bentley
Corniche; Rolls-Royce Camargue
(Camargue, 1975 to date)**
8 cylinders 104.4 × 99mm 6750cc
3 forward speeds (automatic)
wheelbase: 120 inches
number made: still in production
**1977–1980 Rolls-Royce Silver
Shadow II and Bentley T2**
8 cylinders 104.4 × 99mm 6750cc
wheelbase: 120 inches (124 inches
on Silver Wraith II)
**Rolls-Royce Silver
Spirit and Bentley Mulsanne**
8 cylinders 104.4 × 99mm 6750cc
3 forward speeds (automatic)
wheelbase: 120 inches (124 inches
on Silver Spur)
number made: still in production

Index

Eldred who designed it, and Ronald
Watson who compiled the index.

Special credit is due to Nicky Wright
who took most of the photographs,
and to the National Motor Museum,
Beaulieu for providing archival
material.

Thanks are due to the following who
also supplied photographs:
Frank Dale and Stepsons, pages 38, 82
Lawrence Dalton Collection, pages 24,
40, 70, 78, 80
Imperial War Museum, pages 14, 28
National Motor Museum, pages 8, 18,
22, 26, 32, 54, 60, 68, 72
North West Museum of Science &
Technology, page 6
Publifoto, Turin, page 86
Rolls Royce Ltd, pages 10, 26, 76, 84,
86, 92
Salisbury and Winchester Journal,
page 42.

We would also like to thank the
following owners who kindly allowed
their superb automobiles to be
photographed for this book:
Auburn-Cord-Duesenberg Museum
(1931 Springfield Newmarket Brewster
convertible sedan)
Jack Barclay Ltd (1974 Park Ward
Silver Wraith)
P L W Bellin (1958 Silver Wraith
Hooper limousine, 1931 Phantom II
Baker sports saloon)
Leslie Benton (1979 Silver Shadow
saloon)
J W Bowdage (1930 20/25 coupe)
Douglas Bunn (1974 Phantom IV
Mulliner/Park Ward limousine)
Roger Bunn (1928 Phantom I Hooper
saloon)
J J E Clarke (1934 20/25 saloon)
Hermione, Lady Colwyn (Two Silver
Wraith saloons)
Victor Crabb (1911 Silver Ghost tulip
back Lawton limousine, 1930
Phantom II Gill all-weather tourer)
D S Crowther (1933 Phantom II
Hooper Continental sports saloon)
Val Dannevkold (1935 20/25 sedanca
de ville)
H A Edwards (1939 Wraith Park
Ward saloon)
C D Ellis (1929 Phantom I Barker
tourer)
S Fortune (1952 Silver Wraith Hooper
touring limousine)
John Hampton (1950's Bentley R-type
Continental Mulliner coupe, 1925
Silver Ghost Barker tourer)
Hanbury family (1910 40/50 Pullman
limousine)
J L Harvey (1957 Silver Wraith
Hooper limousine)
Harvey Herbert (Corniche coupe)
M J James (1933 20/25 saloon)
Michael M O Jodrell (1933 20/25
close-coupled Hooper sports saloon)
Jack Major (1936 25/30 Thrupp &
Maberly sports limousine)
A W McDowell (1934 20/25 fixed
head coupe)
S R Metcalfe (1935 Bentley 3.5 liter
saloon)
M R Neale (1925 Twenty Flewitt
coupe)
Judge John C North (1946 Silver
Wraith Inskip convertible)
R Pennington (1929 Phantom I
Barker sedanca de ville)
R C Phillips (1956 Silver Cloud I
saloon)
HM The Queen (Phantom IV)
Klaus Riebold (1927 Phantom I
Erdmann & Rossi limousine)
Stanley Sears (1927 Phantom I Clark
sedanca de ville)
John Simonson (1923 fabric saloon)
S M Tidy (1913 Silver Ghost open
drive limousine)
Jack Wahely (1926 Compton 20 drop
head coupe)
Nick Whittaker (1929 Phantom II
sedanca de ville)
John Wise (Silver Cloud Freestone &
Webb drop head coupe)

Author's acknowledgment

I owe a great debt to many people
who have helped to provide
information and photographs for this
book. In particular, Lawrence Dalton
who has lent generously from his own
collection, Dr Robin Barnard who has
made many useful suggestions about
cars and their owners, and Lt Col Eric
Barrass, OBE, Secretary of the Rolls-
Royce Enthusiasts Club. Thanks are
also due to Stewart Daniels, John
Fasal, Bryan Goodman, Roger Hedley,
Keith Marvin, Dennis Miller-Williams
of Rolls-Royce Motors Ltd, W J
Oldham, Major W S Phelps, MVO,
MBE, Superintendent of the Royal
Mews, and Paul Tritton.

Acknowledgments

The publishers would like to thank
Bridget Daly and Richard Nichols for
their help in editing the book, David

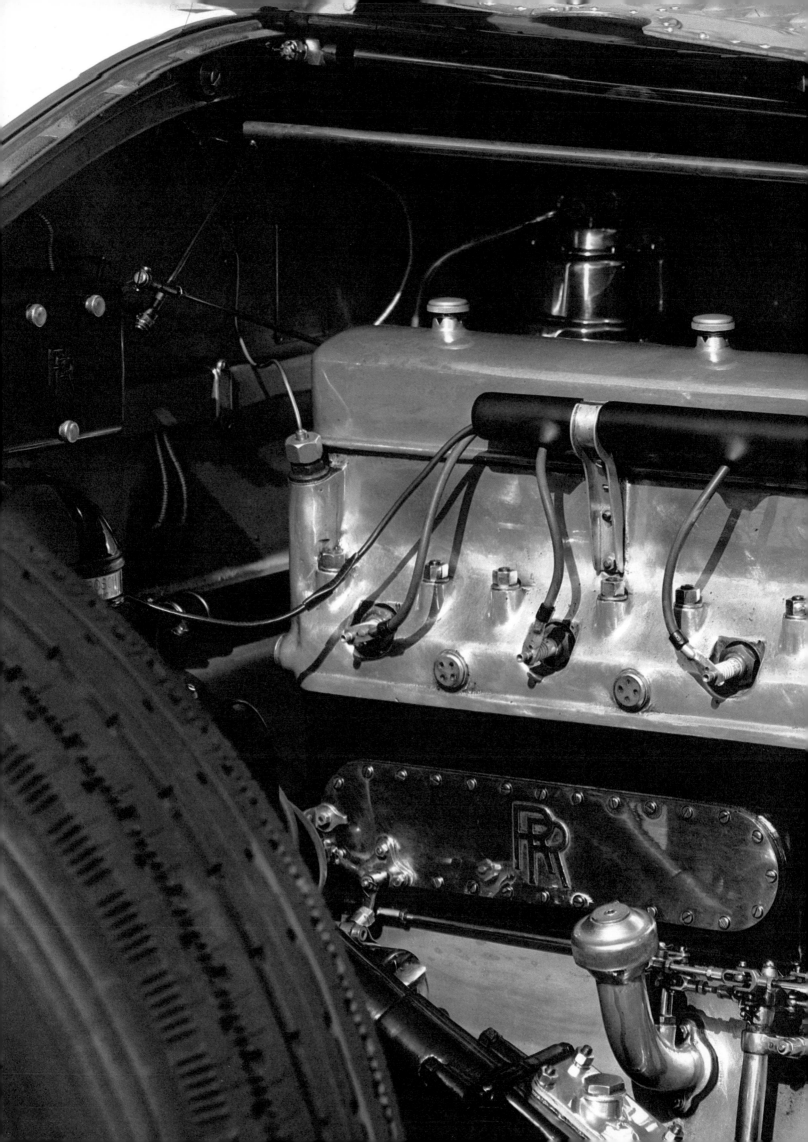